THE *Golden Age* OF YORKSHIRE RAILWAYS

PETER TUFFREY

GREAT N ORTHERN

ACKNOWLEDGEMENTS

I would like to thank the following people for their help:

Paul Bolton; David Burrill; Nick Catford, Disused Stations Website; Neil Cholmondeley; David Clay; Norman Ellis; Peter Jary; David Joy; John Law; Hugh Parkin; Derek Porter, Bill Reed; Andrew Stoppford; Andrew Warnes; Sue Warnes; David Webdale, of Lost Railways of West Yorkshire; Alan Young.

Special thanks are due to my son Tristram for his help and encouragement throughout the project.

PHOTOGRAPHS

Every effort has been made to gain permission to use the photographs in this book. If you feel you have not been contacted please let me know: petertuffrey@rocketmail.com.

INFORMATION

I have taken reasonable steps to verify the accuracy of the information in this book but it may contain errors or omissions. Any information that may be of assistance to rectify any problems will be gratefully received. Please contact me by email: petertuffrey@rocketmail.com – or in writing:
Peter Tuffrey, 8 Wrightson Avenue, Warmsworth, Doncaster, South Yorkshire, DN4 9QL.

Great Northern Books
PO Box 1380, Bradford, BD5 5FB
www.greatnorthernbooks.co.uk

ISBN: 978-1-912101-72-6

Design and layout: David Burrill

CIP Data
A catalogue for this book is available from the British Library

INTRODUCTION
BY DAVID JOY

When was the golden age of Yorkshire railways? There can be no total and exact consensus. To some it will be the 1870s, which saw heroic feats of construction such as the magnificent Settle to Carlisle main line boldly striding over the tops of the Pennines.

To others it will be the late 1930s, when streamlined expresses gave journey times between Leeds and York to London that hitherto had seemed unimaginable. Casting nostalgia and rose-tinted spectacles to one side, there is even an argument that the golden age is now, as the frequency of passenger services has increased to extraordinary new heights.

Yet a true golden age was surely the dawn of the twentieth century in the years between 1900 and the outbreak of World War I. Railways were then in what has succinctly been described as the complacent maturity of their power. Complacent because the advent of competition was scarcely recognized. Little was done to combat the rapid rise of the tramcar, often far more convenient for passengers than stations remote from the places they were supposed to serve. Mature because the network was essentially complete with only a few minor lines still being constructed. Powerful because they held sway in a way that war would change for ever. True, the motor age was not far distant but for the moment the internal combustion engine was seen as something of a joke by most railway companies. That smile would soon be wiped off their faces.

The early years of the twentieth century were also a golden age for photography and especially the picture postcard. Then the equivalent of an email or text message, they were sent in their thousands to nearest and dearest, often featuring a picture of a station as proof of safe arrival. Seen as nothing

special in their day, many have happily survived as images that form a centrepiece of this book.

Although this period forms the core of these pages, a few pictures slip back into the Victorian age and others go forward to the years after World War I. It was an impoverished period for the railways, culminating in the 1923 Grouping of companies which saw Yorkshire shared out between the London Midland & Scottish and the London & North Eastern railways. The LNER inherited the territorial monopoly of the North Eastern Railway that held sway in the North and East Ridings as well as the less urban parts of the West Riding.

In the industrial West Riding it was a different story, where the spoils of wool and especially coal traffic created a unique network divided prior to 1923 between five dominant companies. The Midland, Lancashire & Yorkshire and London & North Western lines went to the LMSR and the Great Northern and Great Central to the LNER. There were also several lesser players and a host of joint lines. The result was much wasteful duplication of facilities but undoubtedly enormous variety and character. It is small wonder that photographs from this area dominate these pages.

At one level the 300-plus illustrations arranged in broadly alphabetical order are a remarkable collection and frequently depict locations – and especially stations – that were seldom photographed. They give a wonderful broad overview of an age long gone but deserve far more careful study.

Take for example the picture on page 7 of Adwick on the West Riding & Grimsby Joint main line between Doncaster and Leeds. The background is a totally rural landscape, which accounts for the various name changes explained in the caption. The station was midway between the villages of Adwick and Carcroft but not especially convenient for either community. The railway therefore presumably went through periods of uncertainty in attempting to please both parties. Be that as it may, the most noticeable feature is the station architecture verging on the bizarre in such a location. The low hipped roofs, bracketed at the eaves, culminate in a conical tower that was topped by a weathervane. It is understandable that the building has survived as a private residence and today there is a more manageable 'basic' station is a little to the south.

It is a busy scene on the Adwick station platform with a group of elegantly dressed ladies perhaps wondering if there was room for all their no doubt voluminous amounts of luggage. There was certainly enough railway staff to help them – and this is a feature apparent in so many of the photographs. One is left with the suspicion that they often spent more time tending station gardens than handling trains, as is evident in the picture of North Grimston, near Malton, which normally saw just six services a day disturbing the rural peace. There was justifiable pride – witness the portico of Cross Gates station almost lost among all its floral glory.

Overall, stations are portrayed in all shapes and sizes. There are the unquestionably magnificent such as Huddersfield and York down to the demure delight of Hayburn Wyke with its single platform set in woodland close to the coast. Some stations and the lines serving them were lost causes virtually from the outset. Take the Nidd Valley Light Railway, opened in such grand style in 1907 that a temperance society vehemently protested about the amount spent on 'intoxicating drinks'. They may have had a point, as in today's money it amounted to over £11,000! Sadly such a glorious start failed to achieve longevity and it carried its last passengers at the end of 1929.

Collectively the photographs provide a fascinating look at railway uniform and how it varied among the different grades. The stationmaster normally stands out to be noticed. He was an important figure in the hierarchy, generally provided with his own house of generous proportions. In the then all-important world of social status, there is a theory that a railway company would assess the size of the local vicarage and ensure that the home provided for the stationmaster was at least as large!

It was still frequently necessary to sit or stand still for the camera, and the choice of location was sometimes surprising. When the eight staff of Wortley station, south of Penistone, posed beneath the 'Gentlemen' toilet sign, it is tempting to wonder if they were making a social statement. They were after all in what was still a man's world and generally had the security of what was often a relatively gentle job for life.

Variety of dress is also evocatively portrayed among the passengers. So much the better when those in the nearby street are also visible, as in the panoramic view of Haworth – the station that came just too late to be used by the Brontë sisters. Arguably best of all are those recording rare occasions when factory workers had time off to go to the seaside. At Morley there was clearly near desperation not to miss an excursion about to depart for Blackpool during the local Feast Holidays. And what a crowd on the edge of the platform in pre Health & Safety days at Southcoates, a suburb of Hull, as a train approaches to take them on an outing to Scarborough. Excitement would know no bounds!

How much of the railway scene they would notice is doubtful, but it was all there to be recorded for posterity in these pictures. On most platforms there would be porters' barrows or handcarts, long bench seating and milk kits. Advertisement hoardings – frequently for Vim and Pears Soap – were prolific. Station bookstalls performed an invaluable service in days long before media saturation. Note the size of the one at Barnsley with its array of newspaper billboards including a headline 'Why Food Is Dearer'. Some problems in life never change!

Stations were lit by lamps that have now become collectors' pieces. Gas was used in the larger towns and cities but elsewhere it was oil with all the labour this involved. It was the same with the essential railway signals, which could sometimes be a dominant feature of the whole scene, as in the magnificent example at Kippax on a minor branch line between Garforth and Castleford. Signalboxes too had great character, their interiors generally polished to perfection as the personal shrine of the signalman.

Immediately outside the station would be an assortment of horse-drawn traps, wagonettes and sundry conveyances plying for hire. There are fine examples in the photographs of Deepcar and the entrance to the up platform at Doncaster, Others can be seen at Driffield, although lurking in the background is future competition in the shape of motorised transport.

Beyond these features seen on almost any railway journey were others not always encountered. In the more hilly reaches of Yorkshire were long tunnels and numerous viaducts, some of which are depicted during construction and one at Penistone after a disastrous collapse. Those travelling in what is now South Yorkshire could scarcely avoid the grime of the vast facilities for coal traffic and the industrial lines serving numerous collieries as well as steelworks. Finally and in a class of its own was the railway town of Doncaster, where pictures of the immense 'Plant' workshops show heavy engineering in its heyday as well as rare glimpses of women at work.

It is all part of the infinite variety that makes the photographs in this book so compelling. They are surely convincing evidence that the early twentieth century was indeed a golden age for Yorkshire railways.

COMPANY ABBREVIATIONS

DVR	Dearne Valley Railway
GCR	Great Central Railway
GNR	Great Northern Railway
H&BR	Hull & Barnsley Railway
H&MR&C	Huddersfield & Manchester Railway & Canal
L&BR	Leeds & Bradford Railway
L&YR	Lancashire & Yorkshire Railway
LMSR	London Midland & Scottish Railway
LNER	London & North Eastern Railway
LNWR	London & North Western Railway
M&LR	Manchester & Leeds Railway
MR	Midland Railway
MS&LR	Manchester, Sheffield & Lincolnshire Railway
NER	North Eastern Railway
NMR	North Midland Railway
NWR	North Western Railway
S&RR	Sheffield & Rotherham Railway
SYR	South Yorkshire Railway
WR&G	West Riding & Grimsby Railway
Y&NMR	York & North Midland Railway

Above and opposite bottom **ADWICK**

The West Riding & Grimsby Railway was a project undertaken by the GN, MS&L and SY railways to join Wakefield to the port of Grimsby. A connection was made between the MS&LR near Stainforth, whilst a branch was formed from the GNR main line north of Doncaster station and joined the new railway just north of Adwick. Here, the only station on the branch was opened on 1st March 1866, initially called Adwick, then early in 1867 changing to Adwick & Carcroft before becoming Adwick-le-Street & Carcroft in March of that year. During 1880 the latter place was given prominence and was placed first in the title and this remained the case until the station closed on 6th November 1967. The building has subsequently become a house, but a new station was opened just to the south of the original on 3rd October 1993. Pictured above is a northbound train of GNR six-wheelers and the image opposite shows the station frontage, which is now quite hidden by a bridge over the main line (left) and a row of large trees (right).

Opposite top **ADDINGHAM**

Signalmen, and perhaps family members of one of the men, pose for the camera outside the signal box at Addingham station. This was located on the Skipton to Ilkley route of the Midland Railway and was opened with the line on 16th May 1888. The signal box, which was located on the eastern side of the station, is of a typical MR design, using wooden boarding throughout for construction and decorated in a shade of yellow with white window frames; 'Addingham' has been fixed to a board using white metal lettering. Both signal box and station were closed in March 1965 as the line was one of the many victims of the 'Beeching Cuts'.

Above **ALNE**

Looking north at Alne station as an up express approaches. The buildings were completely demolished and replaced during the 1930s as this section of the main line was expanded to four tracks.

Below **ALVERTHORPE**

The GNR opened Alverthorpe station on the company's line between Wakefield, Ossett, Dewsbury and Batley in 1872 as there were over 500 people working in a mill nearby. Closure occurred in 1954.

Above and below ANGRAM WATERWORKS

As Bradford grew during the 19th century the demand for water, by both residents and industry, also increased. Engineers turned to various springs, streams and rivers to supply the city and from the mid- to late 1800s several sources were established. In the early 20th century a large-scale project was initiated to obtain water from the Dales through the formation of reservoirs. Angram Reservoir was the second of three established between 1901 and 1936 and was completed around 1915. The Nidd Valley Light Railway was set up by Bradford Waterworks to serve the sites, initially being narrow gauge, but later upgraded to standard. *Angram* - in the top photograph - worked the line during the transition (1907) and moved on soon after.

ARKSEY

The GNR opened Arksey station on 6th June 1848 after the inauguration of the Askern branch, for which the company had running powers. The work was carried out by the Lancashire & Yorkshire Railway and the line met the main line just north of Arksey, having run from Knottingley on the line from Goole to Leeds and Wakefield. Originally known as Stockbridge station, the name change occurred c. 1854 when Arksey was used solely by the GNR. An NER 4-4-0 is seen in charge of the up passenger service. Following closure in 1952, the station was demolished.

Above ARDSLEY STATION AND IRON WORKS

In the mid-1850s two companies sought to join Leeds, Bradford and Wakefield and the two lines subsequently met at Ardsley, where a station was opened in 1857. Both concerns later fell to the GNR. The Yorkshire Iron & Coal Co. works and Ardsley Colliery had rail connections near the station.

Below ARTHINGTON

The Leeds & Thirsk Railway constructed Arthington station (then named Pool) in 1849 as part of the company's route from Leeds to the Stockton & Darlington Railway which opened in sections to 1851. The station only survived for 16 years before being replaced with the buildings pictured here (located just to the south) for the opening of the Otley Branch.

Above **AYSGARTH**

Thoughts of running a line to Aysgarth in the Yorkshire Dales did not come to fruition until the 1870s, when the MR was in the process of building the Settle to Carlisle Railway. The NER, which inherited the main body of track running east of Aysgarth (from the main line at Northallerton) from the York, Newcastle & Berwick Railway (to Bedale) and the Bedale & Leyburn Railway in the late 1850s, decided to take the opportunity to extend the route to meet a branch of the new line at Hawes. Authorisation was given for the project in 1870, but work as far as Askrigg was not completed until 1877 and Aysgarth was open for traffic from 1st February. The building was designed by NER architect Thomas Prosser to the standard H-plan of the period, although stone was used in place of brick. The connection to Hawes was made the following year and the route was subsequently used for excursions to and from the area, which is perhaps the reason for this gathering in the early 20th century. Aysgarth closed in 1964 but there are hopes that the heritage Wensleydale Railway will re-open the section from the current terminus at Redmire to Hawes in order to re-establish this east-west link.

Opposite top and bottom **ARTHINGTON TUNNEL**

The Leeds & Thirsk Railway had several engineering obstacles to overcome before the line could be ready for traffic. The most difficult of these was the rising section of ground between Arthington and Horsforth which prompted the line's engineer Thomas Grainger to drive a tunnel between the two places, measuring just over two miles in length and also commonly known as Bramhope Tunnel. Work began in 1845 and employed over 2,000 up to completion in mid-1849, when 24 of the men had lost their lives in the tunnel. Pictured above is the northern portal at Arthington and below is the southern entrance at Horsforth.

L.S. 37-5. Railway Station, Barnby Don.

Above BARDSEY

A branch between the Leeds to Selby line and the Church Fenton to Harrogate route was proposed in the mid-1860s by the NER. Ten years elapsed before the construction of a single track between Cross Gates and Wetherby was completed with five intermediate stations. One of these was Bardsey, which was the penultimate stop before Wetherby, opened on 1st May 1876. The buildings (of an NER standard design) were on the eastern side of the line, as was a goods yard. At the turn of the century an extra set of tracks was laid throughout the length of the line and the footbridge (seen in the background) was added at this time. Bardsey - and the line - were a victim of the Beeching cuts of the 1960s and closed to passengers in 1964.

Opposite top BAILDON

Station staff and passengers pose for a quick photograph at Baildon as a train approaches from the north. The station was opened by the MR in 1876 with the branch from Shipley to Guiseley. Closed in the 1950s, Baildon was reopened in 1973 for commuter traffic.

Opposite below BARNBY DUN

Barnby Dun station was constructed on the South Yorkshire Railway's line from the GNR's main line at Doncaster to Thorne and later extended to Keadby. Initially, the route was goods only, but a year after opening in 1856 passenger services were added. The line was poorly constructed - no authorising act was obtained - and after amalgamation with the MS&LR in 1864 the line was rebuilt and extended to Barnetby, where a connection was made with the company's main line. Barnby Dun station was one of two of the original stations rebuilt and a new site was chosen which was more advantageous for traffic. This occurred in 1866 and the station lasted over 45 years before being rebuilt for a second time as part of a widening scheme costing £100,000 carried out by the GCR and Barnby Dun is seen here (looking south-west to Doncaster) after the process ended.

Above **BARNOLDSWICK**
MR 0-6-0T no. 1347 stands at the head of a train depositing passengers at Barnoldswick station c. 1900.

Below **BARNSLEY**
The kiosk of once well-known booksellers and newsagents Wyman & Sons Ltd at Barnsley station.

Above **BARTON HILL**

Barton Hill station served the York to Scarborough line for less than 100 years, being closed in 1930.

Below **BARNSLEY**

Locomotives stand outside the engine shed opposite Barnsley station. The building stood from the late 19th century up to 1960 when demolished.

Above BATLEY

Batley station, on the Leeds to Huddersfield line, at the turn of the century. Operated by the LNWR, the company's coaches are in evidence.

Below BEDALE

Bedale station was originally the terminus of a NER single-line branch from Northallerton. Despite a second track being added, the station did not receive another platform.

Above **BERRY BROW**

The Huddersfield & Sheffield Junction Railway was completed in 1850 to Penistone, where a connection was made with the MS&LR. Berry Brow, south of Huddersfield, was the second station on the line and was in use until 1966. A new station bearing the name later opened in 1989.

Below **BIRDWELL & HOYLAND COMMON**

The SYR completed Birdwell & Hoyland Common station as part of the company's line from the Barnsley to Mexborough route and the Sheffield to Rotherham line at Meadowhall.

Above BIRKENSHAW & TONG

The Leeds, Bradford & Halifax Junction Railway was a private enterprise initiated to serve the three places. Soon after the culmination of this work, the company decided to embark on a branch line from the main route between Leeds and Bradford at Laisterdyke to Gildersome by an Act obtained in 1853 just before the opening of the main line the following year. The work took three years and the formal opening took place on 19th August 1856, with the public opening occurring the next day, and directors and guests were treated to luncheon in Bradford, where the party embarked from. At first the branch mainly dealt with goods traffic and Birkenshaw & Tong station was one of two on the line to be provided with a goods shed (the other being Drighlington) and passenger usage was light.

Opposite top BIRKENSHAW & TONG STATION WITH LOCOMOTIVE

GCR Robinson 8N (LNER B6) Class 4-6-0 locomotive no. 5053 - with a very unusually decorated smokebox - pauses at Birkenshaw & Tong station during the LNER period. The engine was constructed at Gorton Works in April 1921 and was the last of the class, which only comprised another two examples. These were similar to the 'Lord Faringdon' Class, but had smaller wheels to allow both passenger and freight duties to be conducted and only two cylinders instead of four. The three locomotives generally stuck together and were allocated to Sheffield, Leeds and Bradford during their working lives. Before Nationalisation in 1948 all had been sent for scrap.

Opposite bottom BINGLEY

Bingley station's history spans 170 years, having been opened in 1847 by the Leeds & Bradford Railway. This concern was backed by the 'Railway King' George Hudson and the company succeeded in constructing a line between the two places (via Shipley) in 1846. In the midst of this project a second scheme was developed whereby a branch would be formed from Shipley to Skipton by way of Keighley. One of the engineering features was Bingley tunnel which measured 151 yards and was passed through just before Bingley station - when travelling in the 'down' direction. The L&BR subsequently became part of the MR and the latter company rebuilt Bingley station in the 1890s. The station is pictured in the early 20th century.

Above BRADFORD EXCHANGE

With the rapid increase in the number of railways during the 1840s came a quick redundancy of facilities. The GNR experienced this with Adolphus Street station in Bradford and reacted by building a link line so that the company's trains could use the L&YR terminus. Bradford Exchange station (off Hall Ings) was opened for traffic in May 1850, but further growth in the railways soon made this inadequate and in the late 1870s the station was demolished and a larger one erected. This had a total of ten platforms split evenly over two sides which were used by the two companies. Aspinall '1400' Class Atlantic no. 1404 stands impatiently on the L&YR's side at the station in the early 1900s.

Opposite top BIRSTWITH

Extending north-west from Harrogate was the Nidd Valley railway, constructed by the NER in the early 1860s. Ultimately, there were several intermediate stations before the terminus at Pateley Bridge but one of the original ones was Birstwith, pictured here with a number of passengers waiting for the next service c. 1910. The station was open until 1951, although freight trains continued to stop there for a further 13 years. After the buildings were demolished during the 1960s, the site was used to build houses.

Opposite bottom BOLTON ABBEY

Staff of Bolton Abbey station happily pose for the camera. For several years the MR line ended at Ilkley before plans were put into place to carry on to Skipton. The new line passed through the lands of the Duke of Devonshire, who made a number of stipulations before he agreed to the project. After opening on 16th May 1888, the line, and particularly Bolton Abbey, became a popular destination for tourists. Royalty also visited on occasion, when guests of the Duke of Devonshire at Bolton Hall

MIDLAND STATION, BRADFORD

MIDLAND RAILWAY STATION · CARRIAGE ENTRANCE · MIDLAND

Above BRADFORD FORSTER SQUARE

NER Fletcher Class 398 0-6-0 locomotive no. 783 stands on the turntable at Bradford Forster Square station. The apparatus was situated a distance away from the station between Trafalgar Street and an overbridge from Snowden Street to Cape Street; the latter feature being visible in the background. No. 783 was erected by Robert Stephenson & Co. in 1872 as part of the first order for 30 engines; the class would total some 318. The type was the NER's main goods locomotive for much of the late 19th century, but only around a quarter remained at Grouping - no. 783 had been scrapped by this time.

Opposite top BRADFORD FORSTER SQUARE

The MR inherited the L&BR's station in Kirkgate during 1853 and was obliged to completely change the facilities in order to keep up with passengers' requirements – echoing the L&YR's experience in the city. Before the end of the 19th century the same action was again necessary and Charles Trubshaw, who designed a number of other stations in Yorkshire, was engaged to produce the plans. The new station had six platforms - at least three are seen here - under an overall roof. At first the station continued to be referred to as Market Street, or 'Midland' as this picture postcard suggests, but subsequently Forster Square was adopted after Grouping, when the facilities were taken over by the LMSR. Recently, the station has undergone another major construction project as the building was demolished during the early 1990s and replaced by a new station on land adjacent.

Opposite bottom BRADFORD MIDLAND HOTEL

As part of the construction of the station in the 1880s, the MR - over five years - built the Midland Hotel and this was also designed by Trubshaw. There were 60 rooms, two large ballrooms, which were said to be particularly impressive, and marble and wooden panelling was used liberally. Many famous people were guests at the hotel and one even died there. Sir Henry Irving, a Shakespearian actor of the 19th century and an inspiration for Bram Stoker's Dracula, collapsed there in 1905 shortly after a performance. At the time of the station's demise the hotel was sold, being subsequently restored, and continues to serve visitors to the city.

MIDLAND RLY EXTENSION TO HUDDERSFIELD "BRADLEY VIADUCTS" No 4

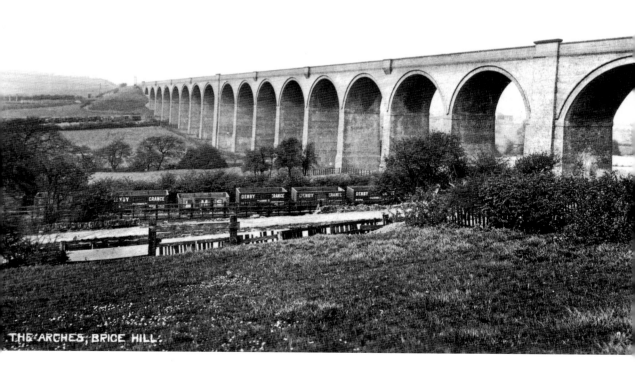

THE ARCHES, BRICE HILL.

Above BRIDLINGTON TURNTABLE

Brute force is used to manoeuvre Gresley K3 Class 2-6-0 locomotive no. 2438 which stands on Bridlington shed's turntable. The engine was one of 20 erected by the North British Locomotive Company's Hyde Park Works, entering traffic in August 1935. Sited on the south side of the shed, the turntable was bought from Cowans Sheldon in 1892 for just under £400 and remained in use, and hand-operated, until the 1960s.

Opposite top BRADLEY VIADUCT MIDLAND RAILWAY EXTENSION

The MR had ambitions to have a presence west of the main line between Sheffield and Leeds and in the second half of the 19th century several attempts were made to bring this into being. After the turn of the century, the MR started work on the project and a line was laid from Royston to Thornhill, south-east of Dewsbury, but the L&YR evidently became nervous of this intrusion into their territory and offered running powers over their lines from there to Halifax. The MR accepted the proposal and further work was abandoned, apart from a branch from Mirfield to Huddersfield which was for goods traffic and the terminus was Newtown Goods Yard. On the approach to the latter a 15-arch viaduct was necessary at Bradley to pass over the River Colne and the Huddersfield Canal. The structure reached up 23 metres from the centre point, was over 230 metres long and used blue bricks. Not being very busy, the branch was shut in the 1960s, but the viaduct remains standing, if somewhat hidden by the growth of trees in the vicinity.

Opposite bottom BRICE HILL, THE ARCHES

A viaduct constructed by the MR on the Royston to Thornhill line was Brice Hill, or Crigglestone, which was located approximately halfway between the two places, just west of Calder Grove, Wakefield. At 387 metres long, the structure straddled several features, such as the L&YR's line from Barnsley, the Horbury and Crigglestone Loop, a private railway for Victoria Colliery and Blacker Beck. As with the abovementioned viaduct, Crigglestone is no longer in use but still stands.

Above **BRAMLEY**

The Leeds, Bradford & Halifax Junction Railway was only independent for two years before amalgamation with the GNR, but the latter had operated the line since opening at the start of August 1854. Bramley station was closed in 1966 and the buildings subsequently demolished. In 1983 services were reinstated with basic facilities offered to travellers.

Below **BROUGH**

Passengers alight from clerestory stock at Brough station at the turn of the century. The Hull & Selby Railway opened the station to passengers in 1840; the NER later assumed responsibility.

Above **BROMPTON**

Brompton station dated from 1854 and was located on the Leeds Northern Railway's extension from Northallerton to Eaglescliffe and the Stockton & Darlington Railway line. Closure occurred in 1965.

Below **BURLEY**

Burley station was opened on the Otley & Ilkley Joint Railway in 1865. The name was altered to Burley-in-Wharfedale in 1922 and has remained in place to the present time.

Above **CASTLEFORD**

GNR Ivatt Class N1 0-6-2T locomotive no. 9440 is pictured at Castleford station c. 1947 with a local passenger train. The engine had only recently received the number and in February 1950 would have BR's '6' prefix added. Withdrawal occurred in March 1957 - a year shy of 50 years in service.

Below **CATCLIFFE**

The Sheffield District Railway had only a short line with two stations, one being Catcliffe, which is seen here, and opened in May 1900. The route was operated by the Lancashire, Derbyshire & East Coast Railway until 1907 when the task was taken over by the GCR. Catcliffe was closed in 1939, although services were reintroduced for a brief period in the late 1940s.

Above **CATTAL**

Thomas Grainger planned the East & West Yorkshire Junction Railway to run between York and Knaresborough. Work began in 1847 with an estimated cost of £200,000 for the 14 miles of double track, stations and viaduct over the River Nidd at Knaresborough. Cattal station was one of several on the line to be ready for traffic in 1848 and these were staffed and operated by the York, Newcastle & Berwick Railway.

Below **CAWOOD**

Cawood station was the terminus for a short light railway branch line from Selby, also serving Wistow and Brayton Gates. NER Worsdell Class H2 locomotive no. 407 is pictured with a service c. 1905; the engine only worked the branch between 1901 and 1908 when replaced by a railcar.

CAWOOD STATION

Above CLAPHAM

Clapham station was opened by the 'Little' North Western Railway in 1849 as part of the company's line from Skipton to Ingleton. The line's services were run by the MR, which later absorbed the company and expanded the line from Clapham to Lancaster and the coast. Clapham remains open, but the facilities have since been reduced and the station house is a private dwelling.

Opposite top CHAPELTOWN

The MR made a gradual approach to Chapeltown. The original section of the route left the company's main line at Wincobank and served foundries in the area. Towards the turn of the century an extension was laid from Chapeltown to Barnsley via Elsecar, providing a slightly shorter route for MR trains north of Sheffield. Chapeltown station opened for passengers on 1st July 1897: in the mid-1980s the facilities were moved a short distance northward.

Opposite bottom CHAPELTOWN & THORNCLIFFE

The South Yorkshire Railway's connecting line from the Sheffield to Rotherham and Barnsley to Mexborough route was almost laid by the MS&LR in the late 1840s, but constant objections from certain parties thwarted the bill. As a result the opportunity was grasped by the SYR and the line was completed in 1854. Chapeltown station was one of several on the line opening their doors to passengers on 4th September, although the event was almost spoiled by the GNR backing out of a proposed takeover of the SYR at the eleventh hour. The latter was required to obtain new locomotives and rolling stock for trains to run and also entered into an agreement with the MR for some trains to be run by the company. The station became Chapeltown & Thorncliffe under the GCR in 1895 and for two years before closure in December 1953 was Chapeltown Central. At the present time the station buildings still stand.

RUNAWAY WRECKAGE AT
CLAYTON WEST
Oct 17 1913

ACCIDENT AT CLECKHEATON
STATION JULY 13 1904
L.V.

Above CLOUGHTON

The Scarborough & Whitby Railway was first proposed in the late 1840s but the adverse terrain and resulting high cost of construction deterred many potential investors from backing the scheme. After finally going ahead in the late 1860s, numerous construction problems were encountered and work had to be abandoned for several years in the late 1870s. The line finally opened in July 1885 with Cloughton as the second stop out of Scarborough. Following the closure of the line in the mid-1960s the station building has become a guest house with an old BR Mark I carriage used for further accommodation, in addition to the old goods shed.

Opposite top CLAYTON WEST

A mishap has occurred at Clayton West on 17th October 1913. A branch from the L&YR's Penistone route served the village - with the station of the same name being the terminus - and Park Mill colliery, which was reached by a spur from the line west of the station; this is perhaps the location for the derailment. October was not a good month for the L&YR's safety record as there was another derailment at Lockwood, close to Huddersfield on the Penistone line. The *Leeds Mercury* of 29th October reported that on the preceding day approx. 30 wagons had become detached from a freight train, which was incidentally heading to Clayton West, and ploughed down a siding into a signal box, then fell 40 ft into Swan Street. Very luckily, the guard in the brake van leapt to safety, as did the signal man and several people in the street below.

Opposite bottom CLECKHEATON ACCIDENT

View south on Tofts Road to Westgate after an accident on 13th July 1905. The West Riding Union Railway planned a line from the line between Bradford and Halifax at Low Moor which was subsequently built and run by the L&YR. Traffic began to run on 18th July 1848, with Cleckheaton Central as one of the stops.

COLLINGHAM STATION

Above and opposite bottom **CONISBROUGH VIADUCT**

The Dearne Valley Railway was promoted at the end of the 19th century to connect the L&YR system from Wakefield to Black Carr Junction south of Doncaster. Work was carried out in sections and Messrs Henry Lovat Ltd were contracted for the last portion from Denaby to Black Carr. This included a viaduct over the River Don at Conisbrough and this was erected by around 250 men between 1906 and 1908. A total of 21 arches - each with a span of 55 ft - connected the two sides of the valley and the centre was 115 ft above the river, which was crossed by an iron bridge. Red bricks faced by blue engineering bricks were used and held together by several thousand tons of cement. The line was opened for mineral and freight traffic in 1909 and passengers from 1912 until September 1951. After closure to the public the line continued with coal trains for a time before final closure in the early 1970s. The viaduct still stands and is now part of the Trans Pennine Trail.

Opposite top **COLLINGHAM BRIDGE**

Collingham Bridge was the last station on the branch connecting the Leeds - Selby and Church Fenton - Harrogate routes. Being only four miles from Harewood House the station attracted aristocracy and royalty on occasion. At the end of April 1904 the *Leeds Mercury* reported that the Prince and Princess of Wales (later King George V and Queen Mary) were to use the station on a private visit to Harewood and to celebrate the occasion Mr Twydale, the stationmaster, had decorated the building with plants and flowers. Four years later the house received King Edward VII, Queen Alexandra and Princess Victoria as part of their visits to Leeds and then Bristol. For this the station had to load and unload three landaus, twenty-five horses and twenty-two servants.

Above **CORNHOLME**

Cornholme station might not have made an appearance in this book if a boundary change had not occurred. Up to this time the village had been located in Lancashire, but in 1888 both Cornholme and Todmorden were taken into the West Riding. The L&YR line had run through the latter for a number of years before the station was opened at Cornholme c. 1878, having been laid by the Manchester & Leeds Railway in the early 1840s. Cornholme had only a brief existence, being closed before the start of the Second World War due to falling passenger numbers, and the buildings were subsequently cleared.

Opposite top **CONISBROUGH**

The South Yorkshire, Doncaster & Goole Railway was promoted in the mid-1840s to form a connection between Doncaster and Barnsley to serve the industrial needs of the area. However, considerations were given to the movement of people and two stations were originally provided when the line opened on 10th November 1849. Conisbrough was one - the other being Doncaster Cherry Lane station. The facilities were quite sparse at this time as Dow in *Great Central Volume One* relates: 'Conisbrough station had a separate Midland booking office [as the company's line between Swinton and Rotherham was taken], and its small, awkwardly arranged wooden buildings included a bare hut as a waiting room.' These persisted for some years until 1883 when the MS&LR spent £2,400 on improvements, which also saw the station moved a few hundred yards to the west.

Opposite bottom **CONONLEY**

Located at the northern end of the Leeds & Bradford Railway's extension to Skipton, the station at Cononley was opened towards the end of 1847. Services were later withdrawn on 22nd March 1965, but reinstated at the end of the 1980s and a station continues to serve the local population and tourists to the area; the buildings and signal box in this image captured in the early 20th century have been demolished.

Above **CROSS GATES**
Station staff proudly pose with a floral advertisement of the places served by Cross Gates station, Leeds.

Opposite top **CRIGGLESTONE**
Crigglestone station was located to the west of the village and was opened by the L&YR in January 1850 on the Wakefield to Barnsley line. The station later had a siding for Crigglestone colliery which was located nearby. From 1924 to 1961 the name was changed to Crigglestone West and at the latter date reverted to the original until closure in 1965. Part of the station remains standing as part of a private residence.

Opposite bottom **CROFTON**
Opened on 1st November 1853, Crofton station served the village four miles to the south of Wakefield on the L&YR's Wakefield to Pontefract line. The cost of running the facilities were evidently not warranted as closure occurred on 30th November 1931. No trace of the station remains.

STATION. CROSSGATES.

P & R.
LEEDS I.

Above CROSS GATES

As opened by the Leeds & Selby Railway c. 1835, Cross Gates station had two platforms, with the booking office and waiting rooms on the north side and just waiting rooms on the south platform. At the turn of the century, Cross Gates was completely remodelled for the increase in running lines, as well as being overdue for better facilities following the opening of the Wetherby branch. The work included moving the station a short distance to the east and increasing the size of the platforms. The main buildings were again on the north side, with waiting rooms on the south. A train - consisting of clerestory stock - is pictured at the station from the footbridge over the lines (with a ramp from Station Road on the right - there was also one to the north platform) before heading into Leeds.

Opposite top CROSS GATES

Interior of one of the station buildings at Cross Gates, c. 1905. A new station was constructed at the turn of the century to improve the facilities on offer. The staff were quite proud of their new buildings and endeavoured to maintain a neat and colourful air for both locals and travellers passing through. To this end, Cross Gates was always well-presented and adorned by plants and flowers, being rewarded on a number of occasions with the title of 'Best Kept Station'.

Opposite below CROSS GATES NORTH JUNCTION

View from Austhorpe Road, Cross Gates, looking west towards the station as a locomotive passes the signal box and takes the line to Selby; on the right is the Wetherby branch.

Above and below CUDWORTH

The North Midland Railway was built in the late 1830s from Derby to Leeds. George Stephenson was the line's engineer and his practice at the time was to plan the route to follow the land which was most favourable. Unfortunately in this instance his line bypassed several important places on the way such as Barnsley and Sheffield. The former was missed by some three miles and the station was built at Cudworth, but was named Barnsley when opening in 1840. Fourteen years later the station was renamed Cudworth for Barnsley and was also rebuilt at this time. In 1870 'for Barnsley' was dropped and the station remained open until 1968. Above is Cudworth station c. 1900, looking south and below is a print of the original NMR Barnsley station.

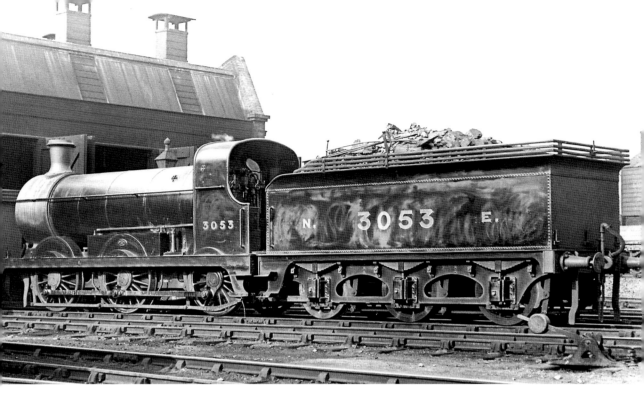

Above **CUDWORTH SHED**

Hull & Barnsley Railway Stirling Class B (LNER J23) 0-6-0 no. 3053 stands outside Cudworth shed c. 1923. The locomotive was part of the first batch built by Kitson & Co. between March and April 1889.

Below **CUDWORTH SHED**

H&BR Stirling J Class (LNER D24) 4-4-0 locomotive no. 2426 was one of only five class members constructed - all at Kitson & Co. in December 1910. The engine is pictured at Cudworth between 1925 and 1930, at which time a domed boiler was fitted.

DALTON MAIN

A number of wagons have come to grief at Dalton Main colliery. The pit was founded in the early 20th century just east of Dalton and Thrybergh. Being close to the MR and GCR lines, Dalton - later renamed Silverwood - had connections to these through the GCR and MR Joint line from Rawmarsh to Braithwell Junction which allowed trains access to the aforementioned companies lines south-east of Sheffield and northward to the GN system.

Above **DACRE**

A goods train is depicted at Dacre station on the line between Harrogate and Pateley Bridge. The station was opened on 1st May 1862 as Dacre Banks and was closed on 2nd April 1951.

Below **DAMEMS**

Opened on 1st September 1867, Damems station was located on the Keighley & Worth Valley Railway and closed 23rd May 1949. The station has since reopened.

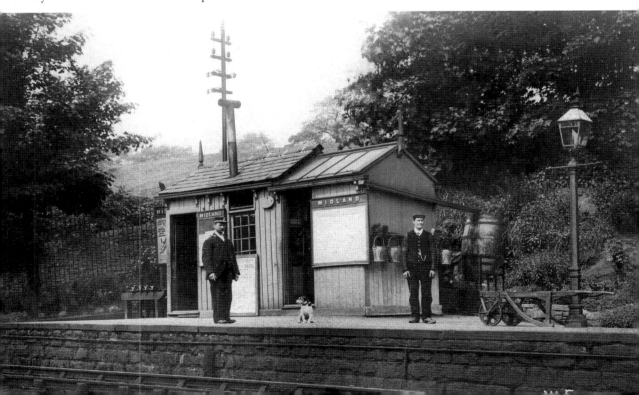

DEEPCAR

To the north-west of Sheffield, Deepcar station was opened on 14th July 1845 by the Sheffield, Ashton-under-Lyne & Manchester Railway as part of the Woodhead route.

Above **DARTON**

The booking office and waiting rooms at Darton station have since been demolished, but the station cottages on the right survive at the present time.

Below **DEEPCAR**

Exterior of Deepcar station, which closed in mid-June 1959. The buildings still stand as a private house.

Above DENABY BRANCH LAND SLIP

On the morning of 24th June 1907, the driver of H&BR Stirling Class B 0-6-0 locomotive no. 96 was travelling along the company's Denaby Branch with a coal train when he noticed a large quantity of soil falling on to the track some 50 yards ahead of him. He quickly applied the brakes and suggested to the fireman that the best course of action would be to alight from the footplate as quickly as possible. Both men did just this and more than likely avoided serious injury. No. 96, which was constructed by the Yorkshire Engine Co. in August 1900, was not too badly damaged and returned to service, later being withdrawn in May 1937.

Opposite top DENABY FOR CONISBOROUGH AND MEXBOROUGH

As the Dearne Valley Railway was primarily built for freight purposes, there was little urgency for passenger services to be offered and when they were, the facilities were extremely basic. One such example was Denaby for Conisborough and Mexborough, opened in mid-1912 as Denaby Halt, and located near to the end of Pastures Road. The change to the first mentioned name occurred c. 1930 and was in use until closure on 1st January 1949.

Opposite below DENBY DALE

The Huddersfield & Sheffield Junction Railway was not an easy undertaking and major engineering features were necessary at several points along the line, two being present near Denby Dale station, pictured. The view has been captured looking north to Wood Lane Bridge, but the scene today is quite unrecognisable with the station buildings demolished and replaced with shelters.

DERWENT VALLEY RAILWAY

The southern half of the Derwent Valley Light Railway was opened to traffic slightly earlier than the date suggested here, but is correct for the whole of the line, running from Cliffe Common to Layerthorpe, York. Worsdell Class 190 (LNER X3) 2-2-4T locomotive no. 1679 started life as a three-cylinder 4-2-0 locomotive in 1846, built by Robert Stephenson & Co. The engine was rebuilt several times subsequently to reach this guise in 1895, remaining in traffic until June 1931, being mainly used for hauling inspection and officers' saloons.

OPENING DERWENT VALLEY LIGHT RAILWAY 19 JULY 1913

Above DENHOLME

The GNR gradually made a line through Denholme from the mid-1870s to mid-1880s as part of a link between the Bradford to Halifax line and Keighley.

Below DENT

Although presently located in Cumbria, Dent had for several centuries belonged to the West Riding of Yorkshire. The station, on the Settle to Carlisle line, has the honour of being the highest in England.

GN RAILWAY DEWSBURY

G N Rly. Station, Dewsbury.

Above DOBCROSS VIADUCT

Soon after the London & North Western Railway was formed in 1846, the company acquired the Huddersfield & Manchester Railway & Canal Co. This concern was formed to link the two places with the help of engineering features of the Huddersfield Narrow Canal because the terrain was especially difficult. Dobcross Viaduct, which is seen from the south looking to Saddleworth station with an LNWR train heading towards Manchester, was just one of the structures built to carry the railway and was completed with the line in 1849.

Opposite top and bottom DEWSBURY (CENTRAL)

In 1871 the GNR was authorised to construct a line from Ossett to Batley by way of Dewsbury. The first section was begun the following year, running from Ossett to Dewsbury with the latter only having a temporary station for opening on 9th September 1874, although freight trains had been operating from 1st May. Deciding not to continue from this point, the GNR let the act to construct the remainder of the line to lapse and new powers had to be obtained in 1877. A further two years passed before work was put in hand and this included the construction of a permanent station at Dewsbury for just over £14,000. This was located a short distance to the north of the temporary facilities, which were subsequently turned into a goods station, and consisted of an island platform raised from the road level; the bridge on the left is passing over Crakenedge Lane. When opened on 12th April 1880 the station was named Dewsbury and not until 1951 was 'Central' added to differentiate from the two other stations in the town. During the cuts of the 1960s, the station was one of two closed and welcomed the last train on 7th September 1964. The frontage seen in the bottom picture has been retained, but the station above has been decimated by the A638, which forms part of the ring road.

DONCASTER

GNR Gresley J22 Class 0-6-0 no. 624 (with LNER '3' prefix denoting the company of origin) takes on water at Doncaster station whilst working a mineral train. The locomotive was built at the town's works in December 1919.

Above **DONCASTER WAGON WORKS**

A number of GNR road vehicles are seen under repair at Doncaster Wagon Works, c. 1910; note the vehicle which has been sent all the way from King's Cross.

Below **DONCASTER**

One of 35 Gresley A4 Class Pacifics built at Doncaster, no. 4496 *Golden Shuttle* was amongst several class members allocated to the LNER's high-speed services, in this instance the 'West Riding Limited'.

Above **DONCASTER WORKS**

From Saturday 26 to Sunday 27 May 1934 Gresley P2 Class 2-8-2 locomotive no. 2001 *Cock o' the North* was the star attraction of Doncaster Works exhibition, which was being held to benefit Doncaster Infirmary and railwaymen's charities. The engine was the latest addition to the LNER's locomotive stock and was both the largest and most powerful passenger engine to be built up to that time. A brief opening ceremony occurred on Saturday and this featured Mr Ronald Matthews (later Sir), who commented that the LNER's Board were 'very proud' of the work Doncaster carried out for the railway and he paid tribute to Mr R.A. Thom and all the staff associated with the works for their service to the company.

Opposite top **DONCASTER WORKS**

When founded in the 1850s, Doncaster Works was a relatively small set of buildings located on the western side of the station. As time progressed, the stock increased both in number and size which required expansions. By the end of the 19th century much of the land west of the station had been occupied and more space was acquired nearby on vacant land to the south west - called the Crimpsall meadows and the GNR's new repair shop took this name. H. Arnold & Son were employed on the building work, which eventually totalled £250,000. The Crimpsall Repair Shop, pictured here c. 1910, had four bays that were 520 ft long by 52 ft wide (served by two 35 ton overhead travelling cranes) and combined could accommodate 100 locomotives. There were also two smaller bays 520 ft by 30 ft used by coppersmiths and fitters to carry out machining and minor boiler repairs. A rail system - of 18-inch gauge - was present inside and outside the shops for the transport of materials. The men were provided with compressed air for powering hand tools, in addition to electricity for some of the machines and the lighting, while heating was provided by hot water pipes.

Opposite below **DONCASTER WORKS**

Women clean carriages at Doncaster during the First World War.

E.L.S. 1-198. Railway Station, Doncaster.

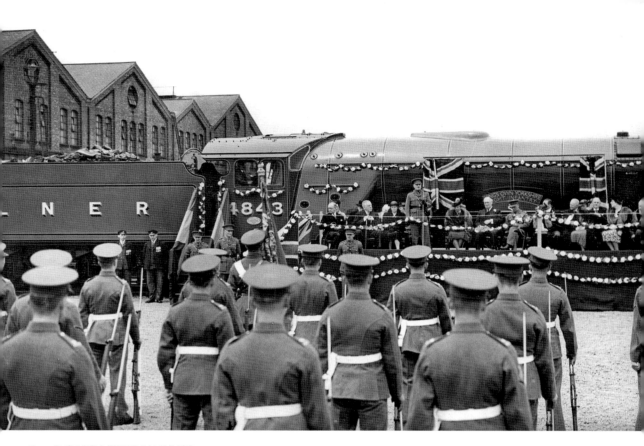

Above **DONCASTER WORKS**

Gresley introduced his V2 Class 2-6-2 for both express passenger and freight services in the mid-1930s. Of the 184 built up to 1944 only 25 were erected at Doncaster and the first of the second batch from the works, which consisted of ten engines, was no. 4843. The locomotive was duly named *King's Own Yorkshire Light Infantry* on 20th May 1939 in a ceremony conducted in the Crimpsall Repair Shop yard. No. 4843 spent almost 25 years working from Doncaster shed, only spending two months away at Grantham in 1961, and the anniversary was prevented by the withdrawal of the engine in September 1963; scrapping was carried out at the works.

Opposite top and bottom **DONCASTER**

A temporary station at Doncaster was opened in 1848. A permanent site was chosen a short distance away at the present location and began serving passengers from September 1850. There was a booking office on the east side and engine shed with associated facilities on the west side of the running lines. Subsequently, as more railway companies served the town, the station was expanded and remodelled, with the first major work taking place in the early 1860s with the goods facilities moved a short distance south and in the 1870s the locomotive shed was demolished and an extensive new depot built, again to the south, at Doncaster Carr. At the station the platforms were improved and lengthened, in addition to new lines being laid. By the turn of the century there were two main platforms - for up and down trains - and a number of bay platforms at either end of the aforementioned. The top picture shows the station frontage before the new building was erected in the early 1940s and the bottom image the up platform from the north end of the down platform.

Left DONCASTER WORKS

A female war worker manoeuvres a wheelset in the Wheel Shop at Doncaster around 1916. After the First World War, H.N. Gresley praised the efforts of the women working at Doncaster Works during the conflict, commenting that he could not speak highly enough of their adaptability in undertaking new tasks.

Below **DONCASTER WORKS**

Gresley B17 Class 4-6-0 no. 2859 *East Anglian* in 2-bay of the Crimpsall Repair Shop. With the success and publicity generated by the A4 Pacifics, the LNER decided to convert two B17s to carry streamlining for the expresses to East Anglia from Liverpool Street. No. 2859 was built at Darlington in June 1936 as *Norwich City* and was modified at Doncaster in September 1937.

DOVECLIFFE G.C. STATION.

Above and below DOVECLIFFE

The South Yorkshire Railway's line between the Sheffield - Rotherham and Doncaster - Barnsley routes also featured Dovecliffe station, which is seen above and below looking south west. When opened on 4th September 1854 the station was known as Smithley, Darley Main & Worsborough, but this was shortened by the end of the decade and over a period of six months was Darcliffe and Darkcliffe before settling on Dovecliffe. The station was closed on 7th December 1953 and the site has since been completely cleared.

Above DRIFFIELD STATION YARD

The Hull & Selby Railway began the process of building a line from Hull to Scarborough in the mid-1840s but this was soon taken over by the Y&NMR. Driffield was one of the stations open for services on 7th October 1846 and was designed by G.T. Andrews. The buildings later received additions such as the canopy seen here, but some original features remain intact at present.

Below DUNFORD BRIDGE

Ivatt C1 Class Atlantic no. 3277 passes through Dunford Bridge station with an express, c. 1927.

Above DUNFORD BRIDGE BOX
Staff pose outside Dunford Bridge signal box, which was located on the station platform.

Below EARLSHEATON
A gathering of GNR station staff and fashionable ladies, c. 1910, at Earlsheaton station, near Dewsbury.

Above ECCLESFIELD

The South Yorkshire Railway opened Ecclesfield station in November 1854 on the branch between the Sheffield and Barnsley lines. Initially being single track, the MS&LR undertook a doubling scheme in the mid-1870s and at this time the station was rebuilt. Situated a short distance north of the original site, the new facilities were ready for services on 1st August 1876. Ecclesfield station was in use until 7th December 1953 and had been known as Ecclesfield East for three years prior to this event.

Opposite top and bottom EASINGWOLD

Fifty years elapsed between the first suggestion of a railway serving Easingwold, north of York, and a scheme being successfully formulated. This was the Easingwold Railway Co. which was a private concern consisting of local landowners and investors who wanted a line to improve their lives. After the act was received the work was put in hand and the two and a half miles of track from Alne on the main line was completed for the official opening on 25th July 1891. The first locomotive was obtained from Hudswell Clarke, Leeds, but was quickly replaced by a new engine, which was an 0-6-0ST instead of an 0-4-0ST originally received, named *Easingwold* (pictured opposite below). In 1903 the aforementioned was sold and replaced by a similar locomotive that carried the name *Easingwold 2* (seen opposite above - with a canine 'cabbing' the engine) and this served the line until 1948. From the turn of the century to the early 1920s old carriages from the North London Railway were used to transport passengers. Easingwold station was closed to passengers shortly after Nationalisation, but remained in use for freight trains until the end of 1957; for the 66 years of operation the line remained privately run.

Above **ELSECAR**

Despite a population of around 2,000 people in the second half of the 19th century, Elsecar had to wait until 1897 before a station was provided on the MR line from Sheffield to Barnsley. The Elsecar branch had entered the area in the early 1850s, but the focus of the line was to serve the local collieries and other industries. Thankfully, the station remains open to serve the local community, albeit without the pleasant station buildings, which are pictured from the south end looking towards Hill Street road bridge.

Opposite top **ECCLESHILL**

The GNR's Eccleshill station was located on the line between Shipley and Laisterdyke and was opened on 15th April 1875. This was some time after freight traffic had begun to run on the route in March 1874 as the main purpose of building the railway was to serve the industries of the area. Nevertheless, nearly £27,000 was spent on constructing stations; the builder employed was T. Whiteley, who used a similar design to the one seen here at Eccleshill at a number of other places. Passenger traffic was not strong enough to keep the station open through the depression years and closure occurred on 2nd February 1931.

Opposite bottom **ELLAND**

Lancashire & Yorkshire Railway staff at Elland station in the early 20th century. On the Manchester & Leeds Railway line, the station was taken over by the L&YR in 1847 and the company subsequently rebuilt the facilities in the late 1860s. Closed in 1962, recently there have been attempts to open a new station to serve the area, but at present these have come to naught.

Above **ESCRICK**
With the reorganisation of the main line in the late 1860s, the NER opened several local stations, one such example being Escrick, seen here, which began life on 2nd January 1871.

Below **EVERINGHAM**
On the Selby to Driffield via Market Weighton line, Everingham station was opened shortly after the line's construction in 1848 as Harswell Gate.

Above and below **FEATHERSTONE**

The Wakefield, Pontefract & Goole Railway was founded in the early 1840s to serve the coalfields in the area by transporting the product to other areas of the country and to the docks for export. By the middle of the decade the company had received authorisation for the line between the three places, in addition to two branches to Arksey and the GNR and Methley and the MR. Featherstone station was built on the main section of the route and was ready for the inauguration on 1st April 1848. The line was subsequently taken over by the L&YR and remains open, although the buildings have been swept away and replaced by shelters.

Above **FERRIBY**

NER Raven S2 Class 4-6-0 no. 819 passes through Ferriby station with a loaded mineral train. The locomotive was one of 20 engines built at Darlington and entered traffic in October 1912.

Below **FERRYBRIDGE**

Ferrybridge station was the last addition to the Swinton & Knottingley Joint line which was a venture promoted by the MR and NER, but also used by several others after completion in 1879. Three years elapsed before Ferrybridge became a stop on the route.

Above **FINNINGLEY**

Despite being closed in 1961, both Finningley station - with platforms - and the signal box remain standing, but the former has become a private dwelling, while the latter remains in use but unmanned to control the level crossing.

Below **FILEY**

NER T.W. Worsdell Class G1 2-4-0 no. 679 is pictured at Filey station c. 1895. The engine was erected at Darlington in December 1887, rebuilt as a 4-4-0 in May 1903 and withdrawn in January 1931.

First Coal drawn from Frickley Pit May 24th, '05.

Above **FRICKLEY**

After a prosperous end to the 19th century the Carlton Main Colliery Co. decided to invest money in a new undertaking to reach the Barnsley seam, which lay under much of South Yorkshire, and was 6 ft thick in the area around Frickley. In March 1903 two shafts were sunk and on 24th May 1905 the seam was reached at 2,004 ft below the surface and the first coal pulled out. Four months later production began and the first trainload left on the MR and NER Swinton & Knottingley line, which ran immediately west of the colliery.

Opposite top **FOGGATHORPE**

There is uncertainty as to when Foggathorpe Gate station opened to passengers, but the date is certainly during 1851 when services were scheduled to stop there. On the Selby to Driffield line, the station had the 'gate' removed from the title from the mid-1860s and was subsequently rebuilt at the end of the 1880s when the line was improved. Being under the ownership of the NER, the style of the station was typical of others from the period and had a booking office and waiting room on the eastern side's ground floor, the remainder of the building being occupied by the stationmaster. Foggathorpe station survived to 1954 for passengers and freight traffic ceased in 1964.

Opposite below **FRIZINGHALL**

The Leeds & Bradford Railway failed to include a station for Frizinghall, two miles north of Bradford, when the route was completed in 1846. The company was subsequently taken over by the MR which added the stop to the line in 1875, serving the local area for close to 100 years before the 'Beeching Cuts' claimed another victim in 1965. However, Frizinghall station was resurrected in 1987 to serve commuters and continues to do so.

Above GOATHLAND

The Whitby & Pickering Railway was an early horse-drawn railway opened in mid-1836 with a small number of intermediate stations, one of these being Goathland. This was at the top of a steep incline that was worked using ropes attached to the carriages and wagons forming the train. Some ten years after opening the route was absorbed by the Y&NMR and steam locomotives began to work the traffic. When the NER took over the railway the decision was taken to divert the line away from the incline and at the same time a new station was built to the design of Thomas Prosser. Ready for service on 1st July 1865, Goathland had 'New Mill' added for a time to recognise the different location and this was in use until the early 1890s. The station has been pictured from a hill on the eastern side looking west to the village.

Opposite top GARFORTH

The Leeds & Selby Railway was authorised in 1830 to connect the textile industry with the River Ouse and from there to the port at Hull. Construction of the route began soon afterwards and was completed in 1834. One of the few original intermediate stations was Garforth, which had a small booking office and waiting room in a modest station house. Minor alterations were made to the facilities in the 1860s before a new station was constructed in 1873 to the plans of architect Thomas Prosser, who designed many stations for the NER.

Opposite bottom GILDERSOME

View from the east side of Gildersome station to the west where the tunnel under the crossroads can be seen. Opened by the GNR on 20th August 1856, the facilities survived until 13th June 1955 and the site has since been completely enveloped by a business park and a roundabout for the A650 and the M621.

GUISELEY

A Midland Railway locomotive with clerestory stock pauses at Guiseley station. The company erected the facilities in 1865.

Above **GOMERSAL**

A late addition to the Yorkshire railway scene was the LNWR relief line from Huddersfield to Leeds opened in October 1900. The intermediate station at Gildersome was closed in October 1953.

Below **GRASSINGTON**

Staff outside the Yorkshire Dales Railway's terminus, Grassington & Threshfield.

Above **HARE PARK & CROFTON**
View west to Hare Park North Junction at Hare Park & Crofton station on the Wakefield to Doncaster line. The former gave a connection to the L&YR line a short distance away.

Below **HAMPOLE**
Also on the former West Riding & Grimsby Railway, shown above, was Hampole, which was added during 1885.

Above **HALIFAX**

L&YR steam railmotor no. 4 is pictured at Halifax station c. 1910 when working services on the Stainland branch. The railmotors were introduced as a cheap way to provide passenger services on sparsely frequented routes and no. 4 was one of eighteen built at Horwich between 1906 and 1911.

Below **HATFIELD & STAINFORTH**

Scene captured from the south end of Hatfield & Stainforth station, looking north towards Hatfield colliery in the distance. The former replaced the SYR's Stainforth station in 1866.

HAWORTH

Following closure in 1962, the line between Keighley and Oxenhope was reopened in 1968 as the Keighley & Worth Valley Railway. Haworth station, and goods yard to the south (right, out of view, in the photograph) has since become the headquarters.

Above **HAWES JUNCTION**

Pictured in the period of the second name, Hawes Junction & Garsdale was opened on 1st August 1876 as Hawes Junction. The LMSR changed the title to Garsdale from 1st September 1932.

Below **HAWES JUNCTION CRASH**

Only three years after a terrible accident which claimed nine lives, another rail crash close to Hawes Junction (5 miles distant from the station) saw the death toll rise to 14 with scores injured. An up Glasgow express stopped on the line with problems raising steam and, despite the best efforts of Guard Whiteley, the following Aberdeen and Edinburgh express ploughed into the rear of the stricken train causing telescoping and a fire.

Above **HAXBY**

Haxby was one of a number of small stations on the York to Scarborough route that was closed on 22 September 1930. The station buildings still stand as a private dwelling.

Below **HAYBURN WYKE**

Hayburn Wyke station (c. 1885 - 1965) on the Scarborough to Whitby line.

Above **HECKMONDWIKE**

Looking south to High Street bridge at Heckmondwike station. Built by the LNWR, the title had 'Spen' added after Grouping and this was used until closure in 1953.

Below **HEALEY HOUSE**

The Meltham branch, running from Lockwood, south of Huddersfield, had two intermediate stations, one being Healey House, opened by the L&YR on 5th July 1869 and closed by BR on 23rd May 1949.

Hellifield Station (1)

Above, below and opposite bottom **HELLIFIELD**

Thankfully, the ornate ironwork present in two of the photographs of Hellifield station survives today and adds character in an otherwise homogenised architectural landscape. The Grade II listed station has recently undergone extensive restoration work for the benefit of future generations.

Opposite above **HEDON**

Hedon station pictured after the Hull to Withernsea line was doubled at the start of the 20th century. Opened by the Hull & Holderness Railway in June 1854, the station survived until October 1964 and goods traffic ceased four years later.

Above **HEMSWORTH BOX**
Hemsworth South signal box controlled traffic moving from the Wakefield to Doncaster line and the H&BR.

Below **HEMSWORTH**
View south east to Hemsworth station, which was located to the north east of the town. Installed on the WR&GR in 1866 the station was subsequently run by the GNR and LNER after Grouping.

Above **HENSALL**

Although the station still serves passengers - on a much reduced basis than in previous years - Hensall station house is privately occupied and has been rendered with the canopy removed.

Below **HICKLETON & THURNSCOE**

From construction to closure, Hickleton & Thurnscoe station only served passengers for 27 years.

Above HOLMES

Holmes station was one of the original stops on the Sheffield & Rotherham Railway's route between the two places, which opened on 1st November 1839. Known as The Holmes for a time, the station served a complex of steel works and rolling mills, as well as a wagon works and pottery factory. Later, there were several junctions close to the station as other railways passed through the area, such as the North Midland Railway and the South Yorkshire Railway; after the former became part of the Midland Railway, the new company took over the S&RR. Holmes station was closed in September 1955 and the buildings sadly demolished; Steel Street crossing still exists and there is a new footbridge over the line.

Opposite top HOLBECK ENGINE SHED

The MR had a nomadic early existence, with regard to locomotive sheds in Leeds. At least three stabled and serviced the company's steeds up to 1866 when a large new facility was erected at Holbeck. This continued the trend of using roundhouses, but in this instance a square building surrounded the turntable and radiating tracks, which could accommodate around 50 locomotives; there were also coaling and repair facilities provided. Arguably, the shed's peak came during the post-Grouping, pre-war period when just over 100 engines were allocated, ranging from humble shunters to large express locomotives, such as Fowler 'Royal Scots' and Stanier 'Jubilees'. One of two engines belonging to the later class is prominent in this image captured from Nineveh Road looking northwards over the site. No. 5621 *Northern Rhodesia* was constructed at Crewe in October 1934 and was allocated to Holbeck from February 1935 to December 1939. After the demise of steam, the shed was demolished and the land transferred for use by diesel locomotives and has further evolved to be involved with the maintenance of DMUs operating in the area.

Opposite below HINDERWELL

On the Saltburn to Whitby line and built by the Whitby, Redcar & Middlesbrough Union Railway in December 1883, Hinderwell station originally only had one platform before receiving a second after the turn of the century. In later years the station building lost the canopy seen here but was otherwise externally unaltered up to closure in 1958. The site has subsequently been cleared and the only remains are the cottages, the gable of which is just visible behind the stone building at the end of the station platform on the left.

Above HOLMFIRTH

A branch line to Holmfirth was constructed at the same time as the route between Huddersfield and Penistone, both tasks being carried out under the guidance of the L&YR. Serving the public between 1850 and 1959, Holmfirth station and branch were closed for two years in the mid-1860s whilst a viaduct was replaced.

Below HORBURY JUNCTION

The L&YR extended their system to cover the area between Wakefield and Barnsley in 1850. Leaving the main line at Horbury, a station was constructed there, on the south east side of the village.

Above **HORBURY**

A L&YR Aspinall 91 Class 0-8-0 locomotive is seen at Horbury with a coal train. The class was designed and introduced at the turn of the century and shared several features with the 1400 Class Atlantics also built at Horwich during this period. A total of 60 0-8-0s were produced up to 1908.

Below **HORTON PARK**

View from Laisteridge Lane bridge looking westward to Horton Park station, with the GNR's City Road branch to the goods station looping away on the right.

Above **HOWDEN**
A local train pauses at Howden station on the Hull to Selby line.

Below **HUDDERSFIELD**
LNWR 0-6-2T no. 1209 as LMSR no. 7722 with six-wheel saloon at Huddersfield station.

Above and below HUDDERSFIELD

The M&LR and H&MR&C entered into a mutually beneficial arrangement to construct a station at Huddersfield in the mid-1840s. Work was not completed on the facilities until 1850, but matters had progressed sufficiently for trains to be accepted there in 1847. The grand frontage was by J.P. Pritchett of York; a second platform with overall roof was added in the mid-1880s.

HULL SPRINGHEAD SHED AND WORKS

As part of the construction of the Hull & Barnsley Railway's system, an engine shed was erected on the north-western outskirts of the city at Springhead. The company was running out of money at this time and thoughts of providing locomotive, carriage and wagons works were not undertaken until later in the decade when an Erecting Shop and ancillary shops were built on the northern side of the engine sheds. At the end of the century a Wagon Shop was in use a short distance to the north east of the aforementioned. After Grouping repairs were limited to minor tasks for engines operating in the area which at this time mainly consisted of ex-NER types, several of which are present in the two interior photographs; a H&BR 0-6-0 stands outside the shed in the other.

Above HUSTHWAITE

Running between Pilmoor and Malton, the NER's line between the two places initially did not serve Husthwaite when laid in 1853, but this was remedied c. 1856 with a single platform and station house, pictured.

Opposite below ILKLEY

Staff at the Otley & Ilkley Joint Railway (NER and MR) station at Ilkley.

Above and below **ILKLEY**

NER Worsdell G5 Class 0-4-4T locomotive no. 1888 was constructed at Darlington Works in December 1896 and was in service until October 1956. Ilkley station was opened in 1865 and was designed by J.H. Sanders, who was employed by the MR.

INGLETON STATION. 538.

KEIGHLEY STATION

Above **KEIGHLEY**

The extension of the Leeds & Bradford Railway was completed in three sections. Firstly, a track was laid between Shipley and Keighley, which was completed in March 1847, then, later in the year, the rails stretched northward to Skipton. Finally, a route taking a south westerly direction ended the project in Colne. The L&BR was absorbed by the MR early in the following decade and in the 1880s the company rebuilt Keighley station.

Opposite above **INGLETON**

The 'Little' North Western Railway was founded in the mid-1840s to form a connection between West Yorkshire and the lines north to Scotland. Originally the proposed route was to run from Skipton via Ingleton and Kirkby Lonsdale to Low Gill where the Lancaster & Carlisle would be used to gain access to the latter. In the event the company only reached as far as Ingleton before the difficulty of constructing the line halted proceedings. The line and station at the latter place was opened for traffic on 30th July 1849, but subsequently the NWR decided to cut across the country to Lancaster and the line from Clapham to Ingleton was closed on 1st June the following year. The NWR was later taken over by the MR and the remainder of the original route was built by the LNWR in the early 1860s. The company opened a new Ingleton station, whilst the MR opted to build their own station, which opened on 1st October 1861 and is pictured here looking south.

Opposite below **JERVAULX**

Stretching over 30 miles between the east coast main line and the Settle to Carlisle route, the Northallerton to Hawes Junction railway was opened in stages. The third part from Bedale to Leyburn featured several intermediate stations including Jervaulx, pictured, which was opened with the line on 19th May 1856, but was named Newton-le-Willows. Renaming to Jervaulx occurred on 1st December 1887 despite being a distance away from the latter mentioned.

Opposite **KILNHURST**

Staff brave the icy platforms at Kilnhurst station,
which was opened by the North Midland
Railway on 6th April 1841 on the line from
Derby to Leeds. Closing a short time later,
reopening occurred in 1852 and Kilnhurst
remained in use until 1968.

Below and opposite below
KILDWICK

The L&BR's line north of Keighley failed to
penetrate several of the villages in the area and
instead passed between them. Shortly after
opening a station was established south of
Kildwick, north-east of Cross Hills and Glusburn
and north-west of Eastburn on the western side
of the road between the latter and Kildwick. This
took the name Kildwick initially before changing
to Kildwick for Cross Hills and Kildwick for
Crosshills. By the time the name had been
settled the MR decided to rebuild the station a
short distance to the west, off the road between
Kildwick and Cross Hills and the task was
completed at the end of the 1880s. The bottom
picture shows the new station, whilst the one
opposite depicts the original while still in use.

Kippax Station. 4063.   Wilkinson Kippax

Above and opposite below **KIPPAX**

View south from Preston Lane (presently Berry Lane) bridge over to Kippax station on the branch between the Leeds and Selby line and the Wakefield to South Milford route via Castleford. Opened on 12th August 1878, Kippax, although closer to Great Preston, served the village south-east of Leeds until 22nd January 1951 when closed due to the coal shortage then being experienced. Freight continued to be collected on the line until the late 1960s and the track was later lifted. Kippax is pictured during a happier time when the station was proudly turned out for the NER's annual 'Best Kept Station' competition and had the honour of being awarded the title.

Opposite above **KINSLEY BRIDGE**

View south-west as a GNR 0-6-0 - with Ivatt lineage - passes over Hoyle Mill Road bridge, which was located to the west of Hemsworth station at Kinsley, on the West Riding & Grimsby line. The coal train had perhaps been attached to the engine at Hemsworth colliery which was located only a short distance away.

Left KIRKBY MOORSIDE

The NER took the liberty of changing the spelling of the market town of Kirkbymoorside, North Yorkshire, to 'Kirby Moorside' and this was in use from opening on 1st January 1874 to closure on 2nd February 1953. The reason for this change is unknown.

Opposite below KIRK SMEATON

Scene captured from the south-west end of Kirk Smeaton station. The Hull & Barnsley Railway line left the latter location before cutting across the rural area north of Doncaster to Hull. When leaving the Barnsley area, the line skirted past the edge of Kirk Smeaton and Little Smeaton and to serve the two places the aforementioned station was opened on 27th July 1885, remaining so until 1st January 1932.

Below KIRKHEATON

The LNWR did not manage to penetrate into South Yorkshire and the farthest the company went was Kirkburton, which was the terminus for the branch of the same name. One of the stations on this line was Kirkheaton, opened on 7th October 1867 and closed in July 1930; goods traffic lingered on until the 1960s.

Above KIRKSTALL

An air of pleasantness surrounds Kirkstall station as Kirkstall Abbey provides an interesting backdrop for passengers either waiting or passing through. The abbey dates from the 12th century and was bequeathed to Leeds Council in the late 19th century by wealthy businessman John Thomas North. Kirkstall station was rebuilt in 1905, replacing a station from 1846.

A busy gang of workers at the East June Ldyke. July 3rd 1921

Above, below and opposite below **LAISTERDYKE**

A set of post cards document the track work carried out at Laisterdyke East Junction in the early 1920s. The work is concentrated on the line to Low Moor via Dudley Hill, whilst the main line from Leeds to Bradford is on the left hand side. The junction was a short distance away from Laisterdyke station.

Lifting Permanent Way at the East June Laisterdyke GNR. July 3rd 1921 190¾ to 19½ miles.

London & North Eastern Railway Gresley 4-6-4 no. 10000 is pictured departing from Leeds New station with an unidentified express passenger service on 7th July 1930. The locomotive was the culmination of several years' design work which aimed to reduce coal consumption through the use of a high-pressure boiler - in this instance 450 lb per sq. in. - as favourable results had been obtained in marine applications. Gresley approached Yarrow & Co., Glasgow, to manufacture the boiler, which was an unusual shape giving rise to several unflattering sobriquets in later years, and this was fitted to a chassis similar to the LNER's contemporary Pacific Class engines. Entering traffic in late 1929 no. 10000 spent a long time under test from Darlington (where final assembly took place) and some of the trains worked included expresses between Newcastle and Leeds. The water tube boiler was later removed and a conventional boiler fitted during 1937. No. 10000, later BR no. 60700, ran in this form until withdrawn in June 1959.

Above LEEDS CENTRAL

During the mid-1930s several railway companies across the globe made efforts to entice passengers by offering high-speed services. The 'West Riding Limited' was one of several offered by the LNER during this period and was scheduled to run the Leeds - King's Cross section non-stop in 2 hours 45 minutes at an average speed of 68 m.p.h. The departure time at Bradford was 11.10 but the train headed from there behind specially prepared N2 Class 0-6-2T engines before being attached to an A4 to leave Leeds at 11.33. The return service was a late departure with a slot booked out of King's Cross for 19.10 and heading north with an expected average speed of 68.5 m.p.h. The press demonstration (pictured) took place on Thursday, 23rd September, leaving Bradford at 14.18 and Leeds 14.45 to travel to Barkston, Lincolnshire, in 77 minutes for the 75½ miles from Leeds. A4 Class Pacific no. 4495 *Golden Fleece* was at the head of the train with Driver J. Sherriff at the controls and Fireman Schofield with the shovel; both men were from Doncaster shed. No extraordinarily high speeds were attempted as had been the case with a number of demonstrations by the company previously, but the crew had the train running at 93 m.p.h. past Crow Park on the first leg. At Barkston the Lord Mayor of Leeds, Ald. Tom Coombs, was taken to the footplate by Doncaster Mechanical Engineer , Mr R.A. Thom, who is seen here looking at the camera with white paper in his hand.

Above LEEDS WELLINGTON

MR S.W. Johnson Class 1532 0-4-4T locomotive no. 1546 stands at Leeds Wellington station, alongside Leeds New station, with a train comprising clerestory stock. The engine was one of 65 built to the design at Derby Works between 1881 and 1886, appearing as part of the first batch of 20, being amongst those not fitted with condensing apparatus. No. 1546 worked from Bradford for a number of years and was withdrawn in April 1924.

Opposite top LEEDS WELLINGTON

The North Midland Railway terminus was established at Hunslet Lane and began to accept traffic on 1st July 1840. The location, which was south of the centre of the city, was soon deemed undesirable and an extension of the line was made to the eastern end of Wellington Street, where several other thoroughfares converged. A temporary structure was put into use on 1st July 1846 before Wellington station proper was ready on 1st October 1850, with four platforms. Whilst subsequent increases in traffic led to extensions, the station remained a modest affair, as is demonstrated by the frontage, which is decorated to celebrate the 300th anniversary of the granting of a municipal charter to Leeds.

Opposite below LEEDS CENTRAL

Several early railway companies entered into an agreement to share a station that was accessed from Wellington Street, being a short distance to the west of the MR establishment. Like the aforementioned, this was at first only to be a temporary arrangement but the will was lacking for progress to be made and in later years Leeds Central station became the home of the GNR and L&YR after the LNWR and NER departed for pastures new. After Grouping the LNER became the majority shareholder, even though the LMSR had running powers into the station. Ex-GNR Ivatt Atlantic no. 3274 is ready to depart with a Pullman service c. 1930.

Below **LEEDS NEW**

NER W. Worsdell Class M 4-4-0 no. 1619 was the sole representative of the design to use compound working. This arrangement had been favoured by Worsdell's brother and predecessor T.W. Worsdell, though after the succession, compound working was gradually phased out on NER locomotives. Nevertheless, no. 1619 was said to be a very capable engine from when built at Gateshead in May 1893 with two compound cylinders and after rebuilding in 1898 with three. At this time the locomotive was moved to Leeds to work expresses north and is pictured here at Leeds New station with one to Edinburgh, c. 1900, although the train would probably only be taken as far as Newcastle. Leeds New station was the result of a connection between the North Eastern Railway's old station at Marsh Lane and the London & North Western Railway line at Leeds Junction. Both companies were involved in the construction of the station, which initially only had three platforms when opened to traffic on 1st April 1869. By the time of its combination with Leeds Wellington station on 2nd May 1938 ten platforms were in use and the name was then changed to Leeds City.

THE QUICKEST TRAIN IN EUROPE. NORTH EASTERN 8·50. A.M. LEEDS TO EDINBURGH

Above **LIGHTCLIFFE**

L&YR Aspinall 1008 Class 2-4-2T engine pauses at Lightcliffe station, on the Halifax to Bradford line, with a local service. The company opened the station on 7th August 1850 and the facilities later fell victim to the 'Beeching Axe', closing on 14th June 1965. The buildings have since been demolished.

EW STATION, LEEDS. 560 / 408

Above LEEDS NEW

Scene captured on the platforms of Leeds New Station. Despite the erection of the Queen's Hotel in the late 1930s, the station was little altered until the major rebuilding work of the 1960s when the train shed was demolished and a new one built.

Below LIVERSEDGE

View northwest towards the short tunnel at Knowler Hill from Liversedge station. Located on the L&YR's line to Mirfield, the facilities were operational between 1848 and 1965; only the tunnel remains.

STATION LOFTHOUSE 56

Above **LOFTHOUSE-IN-NIDDERDALE**
Built by Kerr, Stuart & Co. for the Great Western Railway in 1905, this railcar was deemed surplus to requirements in 1920 and was bought to work on the Nidd Valley Light Railway and did so for many years.

Below **LOFTHOUSE-IN-NIDDERDALE**
Official opening of Lofthouse station on the Nidd Valley line on 12th September 1907.

Above **LOFTHOUSE**

View north to Lingwell Lane bridge over the line between Wakefield and Leeds, which featured Lofthouse station - seen here. Opened c. 1858 as Lofthouse the name subsequently had Outwood added; closure occurred in 1960. A new station was opened in the area in 1988 and was situated on the opposite side of the bridge. Another Lofthouse station was opened in 1876 by the Methley Joint Railway, which was a concern established by several companies, and this was also named Lofthouse & Outwood from the early 20th century until closure in 1957.

Opposite top **LOVERSALL RAILWAY LINE CONSTRUCTION**

Work pauses for this picture to be taken, showing men, horse and steam excavator in a cutting on the Dearne Valley Railway line near Loversall, south of Doncaster, close to the route's junction with the GNR main line at Black Carr. The DVR let three companies take up the task of laying the rails which meant that the line was built in three sections, with the cutting at Loversall being on the final part from Cadeby to Black Carr. H. Lovatt Ltd won the contract for this section in 1904, but owing to the land the work was not completed until 1909.

Opposite below **MALTBY NEW RAILWAY**

All of the major railways running around South Yorkshire at the turn of the century were interested in establishing a presence in the south-east of the area, near to the border with Nottinghamshire. As some schemes failed to gain the necessary support and others did not get further than a proposal, the railway companies - GCR, GNR, L&YR, MR and NER - joined forces to build a joint line from Dinnington to Kirk Sandall, just north east of Doncaster, beginning in late 1905. About halfway along the route was Maltby where a colliery was sunk in 1907 and benefiting from the newly laid railway. Work is seen progressing through the bedrock at Maltby as the spoil from the steam excavators (seen in the distance) is removed by one of the hundreds of wagons used by contractors Whittaker Bros, Leeds.

NEW RAILWAY, MALTBY.

L.M.S. Station, Methley. 1925.

Above **METHLEY**

Looking east at Methley station, c. 1925. This was the first to carry the name as two others were subsequently installed a distance to the south, although none were actually located in the area considered to be Methley village. The station was built by the North Midland Railway, on the route from Derby to Leeds, and opened on 6th April 1841. The L&YR was the next to open a station - Methley Junction - c. 1860 near the connection with the aforementioned line, being the end of the company's line from Knottingley. In mid-1869 the Methley Joint Railway opened the third station on the curve connecting the line from Lofthouse to the L&YR; a distinction between the NMR station and the latter was not made until after Nationalisation when they became Methley North and Methley South respectively. The former closed on 16th September 1957, having been preceded by Methley Junction during the Second World War, and was followed by Methley South in 1960. Methley North station house survives today as a private residence, whilst the Station Road level crossing - the location where this picture was taken - has been gated off.

Opposite top and bottom **MASHAM**

Two views of Masham station, which was the terminus for the branch from Melmerby on the line between Harrogate and Northallerton. The Masham line was constructed by the NER between 1873 and 1875, being ready for traffic on 10th June. The station consisted of waiting room and ticket office (right side, top picture), station master's house (centre) and lavatories (left). From opening there were less than five passenger trains daily, with moderate freight traffic, and with the rise of the motor car patronage declined during the 1920s leading to the removal of passenger services on 1st January 1931; goods trains continued to run through to late 1963. Masham station still stands as a private dwelling, whilst the land surrounding, which formed the goods yard, has been turned into a camping and caravan park.

Below MEXBOROUGH SHED

The South Yorkshire Railway installed a one-track engine shed on the north side of the Barnsley to Mexborough line (near the junction with the MR line) in 1847 and this was subsequently replaced, some ten years later, by a larger building on the opposite side of the line. In the early 1870s the MS&LR extended the line from Rotherham to Mexborough, joining the aforementioned route a short distance to the east of the engine shed. Soon after this work was carried out a large new engine shed was built. This is the location of GCR Robinson Class 9J (LNER J11) 0-6-0 no. 1049, which was constructed by Neilson, Reid & Co. in October 1902 and withdrawn in August 1955. Mexborough shed closed in 1964 and the site was later cleared, making way for an industrial estate.

Above **MEXBOROUGH**

Shortly after the completion of the first section of the SYR's line between Doncaster and Barnsley - from Doncaster to Swinton - Mexborough Junction station was opened in early 1850 to the south of the settlement across the River Don. Like Mexborough engine shed, the station was affected by the construction of the line from Rotherham and was moved to a new position west, on the opposite side of the river. Receiving the first passengers on 3rd April 1871, the station continues to serve the town; the buildings seen here remain in railway use.

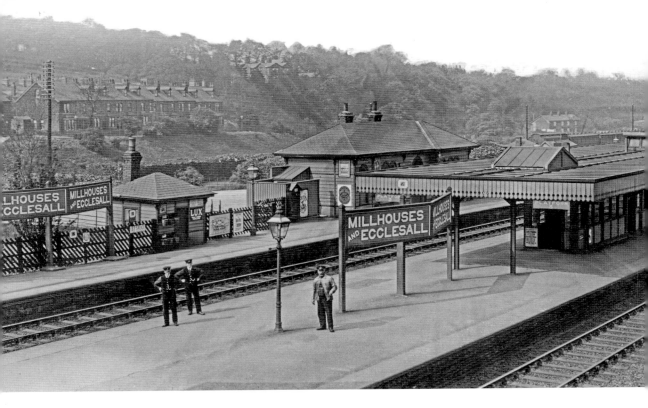

Above MILLHOUSES & ECCLESALL

After opening on 1st February 1870 as Ecclesall, the station, which was built by the MR on the route from Chesterfield to Rotherham via Sheffield, went through several combinations of the title with Millhouses.

Below MORLEY

Passengers rush to board a train ready to depart from the LNWR's Morley station. This postcard view bears the inscription 'Blackpool Excursion Morley Feast Holidays'.

Above MYTHOLMROYD

For the sake of public safety, workers fence off the edges of Mytholmroyd station, on the Manchester to Leeds line, as the platforms were located on a viaduct. The station building (centre) was three storeys high and led down to street level.

Below NETHERTON

View north to Huddersfield at Netherton station on the Meltham branch.

The Station, Normanto

Above **NORTH GRIMSTON**

Staff and excursionists enjoy the floral arrangements at North Grimston station. In the mid-1930s the LNER advertised excursions from places such as Leeds and Hull to Bridlington and Scarborough which also called at stations such as North Grimston and Settrington - on the Malton to Driffield line - for passengers to see the flowers. Both were often entered into the company's 'Best Kept Station' competition, the latter winning for several successive years and North Grimston taking a Class B prize (of £5) in 1939, also being amongst a number given a First Class award in 1929.

Opposite top and bottom **NORMANTON**

The small town of Normanton experienced a largely unexpected period of growth during the 1840s and 1850s thanks to the arrival of several important railways in the area. Firstly, there was the North Midland Railway, then the York & North Midland formed a junction with the line just to the north, allowing traffic to run through from York and Selby and finally, the Manchester & Leeds Railway connected to the south. All three contributed to the cost of the station, but the traffic subsequently demanded that improved facilities be offered to passengers and these were completed c. 1845 to the designs of G.T. Andrews - the picture opposite below dates from this period. In the mid-1860s this was swept away by new buildings grouped on a single island platform, with central waiting area, etc. Unfortunately, the station's active role in the network declined towards the close of the 19th century and continued to do so through to the 1960s. Normanton station has since been demolished and only the platforms remain, being surrounded by overgrown former sidings.

Above **NEEPSEND SHED**
GCR Robinson 11B Class (LNER D9) 4-4-0 no. 1026 (as LNER no. 6026) with crew at Neepsend shed, Sheffield. The locomotive was in service between March 1902 and July 1949.

Below **NORTON**
View north to Norton station on the Doncaster to Knottingley line. Closed on 10th March 1947, the station house (left) still survives but the crossing house has been replaced by a signal box.

Above **NOSTELL**
Two groups of soldiers line up for this photograph, taken at Nostell station c. 1910.

Below **NOTTON**
Originally just Notton when opened by the MS&LR on 1st September 1882, the station was renamed Notton & Royston by the company on 1st December 1896.

Below OAKWORTH

Staff at Oakworth station on the Keighley &
Worth Valley Railway pose for the camera, c.
1910. Built in 1867 the station was in use
until 1962 and apart from accepting
passengers, also handled freight, which was
mainly livestock, there being a 5-ton crane
and goods shed (seen in the distance on the
left). The signal box controlled the goods
yard and the passing loop (track on right)
until the late 1950s when they were deemed
surplus to requirements and the box was later
demolished. Oakworth reopened a short time
after the other stations on the line and was
subsequently restored reflecting the station at
the turn of the century. As a result Oakworth
was used as a backdrop for the popular film,
The Railway Children.

Above **NUNBURNHOLME**

The Y&NMR was authorised to construct a line from York to Beverley in 1846 and the task initially went so smoothly that the track had been laid as far as Market Weighton by the end of 1847. The intermediate station of Burnby had appeared in the timetable by mid-1848. The station was designed by G.T. Andrews and had the stationmaster's house joined with the passenger facilities. From the beginning of 1873 the name was changed from Burnby to Nunburnholme and this remained in use until closure on 1st April 1951.

Above OSSETT
View south from Station Road bridge to Ossett station, showing the goods yard on the western side.

Below OVENDEN
Ovenden station on the Halifax & Ovenden Junction Railway, a GNR and L&YR joint line, looking north.

Above **OTLEY**

A train of NER stock pauses at Otley station, jointly run by the company and the MR.

Below **OSSETT**

GNR railcar no. 7 stands against the backdrop of Ossett Congregational Church, which has now been demolished, as has the station, both being replaced by housing.

Above **PARKGATE & RAWMARSH**
Looking north with Aldwarke Main Colliery on the right; Parkgate steel works was on the south west side.

Below **PARKGATE**
0-4-0ST locomotive no. 22 at work for the Park Gate Iron & Steel Co., which was founded in the 1820s.

Above **PATELEY BRIDGE**
The terminus for the NER's Nidd Valley branch, Pateley Bridge station.

Below **PATELEY BRIDGE**
The Nidd Valley Light Railway began at a different Pateley Bridge station, which was a short distance to the north west of the above mentioned.

The Station Pateley Bridge.

Penistone Station

Above **PENISTONE**

The original station at Penistone was opened by the MS&LR on 14th July 1845 at the end of St Mary's Lane, now Bridge Street. For a time afterwards the name also contained reference to the nearby village of Thurlstone. After the arrival of the H&SJR, which was later absorbed by the L&YR, in 1850, trains had to travel a short distance to the west along MS&LR metals to gain access to Penistone station. This persisted for a number of years until the early 1870s when a new station was constructed on the junction, with the MS&LR occupying the south west side with an island platform and the L&YR had a single platform on the west side of the line from the viaduct. The picture has been taken looking to the south (the Yorkshire Steel & Iron Co. is prominently featured) from the MS&LR side, now GCR which is displayed on the sides of the carriages and express locomotives.

Opposite above **PATELEY BRIDGE**

Another view of the NER's Pateley Bridge station. Opened on 1st May 1862, traffic had declined to such an extent that closure to passengers was necessary in April 1951, although freight lingered on until the early 1960s. The lines were subsequently lifted and the station has become a private residence.

Opposite below **PENISTONE**

Picture taken from the west end of Penistone station. At the platform is MS&LR Parker Class 3 (LNER F1) 2-4-2T no. 736 which was erected by Neilson & Co. in July 1892. The design was produced to handle the suburban passenger traffic around Manchester, so no. 736 being pictured at Penistone is perhaps a little unusual, although the engine was one of several class members built with an increased coal capacity - 3 tons 5 cwt against 3 tons for the majority. No. 736 is also photographed before having a Belpaire firebox fitted; this task was carried out between 1910 and 1923. The locomotive was condemned in 1937.

WENTWORTH ARMS HOTEL BOWLING GREEN
PENISTONE

PENISTONE VIADUCT WRECK, FEB 2ND 1916. NO1

Above PONTEFRACT, BAGHILL

Lying on the eastern side of Pontefract, Baghill station was the last of three stations built to serve the town. Opened by the MR and NER on the Swinton & Knottingley Joint line from 1st July 1879, the station was preceded by Monkhill (1848) and Tanshelf (1871). Initially, Baghill was known as Pontefract New station, but the former was adopted relatively soon after, even if not officially until the 1930s. Incredibly, all three stations remain open, although Baghill only receives four passenger trains a day. The picture was taken from the station's east side, looking west up Station Road. Baghill is little altered, apart from the loss of the chimney stacks and canopy.

Opposite above PENISTONE VIADUCT

The Huddersfield & Sheffield Junction Railway left the Manchester to Leeds line west of the former town and headed south east to Penistone where a connection was formed with the MS&LR. The bleak terrain along the route of the railway meant that several bridges, tunnels and viaducts were necessary. Of the latter there were a total of four: Paddock; Lockwood; Denby Dale; Penistone. The last mentioned was not the tallest at only 83 ft above the River Don, but was quite long, measuring 330 yards with 29 arches; the viaduct also curved at a radius of 40 chains from the embankment (600 yards long) on the north side of the valley to the south end.

Opposite below PENISTONE VIADUCT WRECK

On 2nd February 1916 the mid-afternoon service from Huddersfield had just arrived at Penistone station and the locomotive, Aspinall 2-4-2T no. 661, was engaged on shunting duties before returning north with the 16.40 train, which was usually busy with schoolboys from Penistone Grammar. Upon passing on to the viaduct the driver, George Lockwood, felt the track and engine sink down at which point both he and the fireman alighted from the footplate just before the entire section surrounding the second pier collapsed into the River Don below. A week earlier a disturbance in the masonry in this area had been discovered and work was progressing to correct the defect at this time; luckily the men employed in the area saw falling stones and were a safe distance away when the collapse occurred. The L&YR moved quickly to rebuild and the task was completed by mid-August, with large quantities of concrete being used to reinforce the foundations. Unfortunately, one workman, Edmund Peel, was killed in March when stones being lifted fell and struck him on the head.

Above **PONTEFRACT TANSHELF**

L&YR Aspinall 1008 Class 2-4-2T locomotive no. 1388 - as LMSR no. 10804 - is at Pontefract Tanshelf station with a local passenger service. Tanshelf was opened on the L&YR's Wakefield to Pontefract line on 17th July 1871 and was later closed on 2nd January 1967, only to be resurrected in 1992. No. 10804 was built in July 1898 and was withdrawn in February 1950.

Below **PORTSMOUTH**

The landlocked Portsmouth, north of Todmorden and just west of Cornholme. The village was previously in Lancashire, but boundary changes placed the area in the West Riding during the 1880s. Portsmouth station was opened by the Manchester & Leeds Railway c. 1850 and closure occurred in 1958.

Above **PUDSEY LOWTOWN**

The GNR made a foray into providing new suburban services in the 1870s and one scheme was the Pudsey Loop, which branched off the Leeds to Bradford line east of Stanningley to head back west to Pudsey where two stations were erected – one being Lowtown, the other Greenside was the terminus until 1893. Both were active from 1878 until 1964 when the route closed.

Below **QUEENSBURY**

Queensbury was another GNR station opened in the late 1870s, but closure occurred in 1955.

RAMSGILL STATION N.V.L.R.

S. 142-21. RAILWAY STATION, RAWCLIFFE.

Above **RIBBLEHEAD**

An engineer's train clears the drifts from the line around Ribblehead station and pauses there for a break in proceedings. Given the position of the station on the moors of the Yorkshire Dales, notes on the weather were at one time made by station staff. The MR built the station on the company's Settle to Carlisle route, being ready for traffic on 4th December 1876 as Batty Green, but was renamed the following year. Shut in 1970, Ribblehead station re-emerged as part of the fight to stop the Settle and Carlisle route from closure and has since been restored by the Settle & Carlisle Railway Trust.

Opposite above **RAMSGILL**

The former stations of the Nidd Valley Light Railway have several similarities, one of these being the design as both Pateley Bridge and Lofthouse bear more than a passing resemblance. All were also open for only a brief period and have since become private residences.

Opposite below **RAWCLIFFE**

Rawcliffe station was one of the original stops on the Wakefield, Pontefract & Goole Railway when completed in 1848. The station, west of Goole, has been photographed by eminent Doncaster-based photographer Edgar Leonard Scrivens looking towards the first-mentioned town and Bridge Lane level crossing. Rawcliffe remains open but the station house has entered private hands.

RILLINGTON. RAILWAY STATION.

Above **ROSSINGTON**

Rossington station on the GNR main line south of Doncaster. The station was situated on the west side of the village, but after the sinking of the colliery also served New Rossington which was laid out further to the west. Opened on 4th September 1849, closure occurred on 6th October 1958. Rossington is seen looking south with the goods yard in the distance; the station house still stands as a dwelling, whilst the rest has disappeared.

Opposite above **ROTHER VALE COLLIERIES LTD LOCOMOTIVE**

Beyer Peacock-built 0-6-0ST *Rothervale No. 0*. The locomotive was built in the late 1870s and was acquired by Rother Vale Collieries Ltd in 1890, mainly working at Treeton colliery until scrapped in the late 1950s.

Opposite below **RILLINGTON**

The York & North Midland Railway was authorised to construct a branch from the York to Scarborough line to Pickering and onwards to Whitby. The connection to Pickering was started at Rillington where a station was opened on 8th July 1845. Designed by G.T. Andrews, the trainshed was an addition around two years after opening. Rillington was closed in 1930 and the trainshed fell into a state of disrepair before being demolished, although the main station building (out of view on the right) remains standing.

MASBRO STATION.
S. W. & S.

NO 3. ROTHERHAM "TERRIERS" OFF TO CAMP AUG. 2ND 1908.

Above RUSWARP

View west at Ruswarp station, west of Whitby on the line from Pickering, towards High Street level crossing and the bridge over the River Esk. Built in the late 1840s the station remains open, but is now on the line from Middlesbrough.

Opposite above ROTHERHAM MASBOROUGH

George Stephenson followed the 'path of least resistance' when surveying routes for railways. This had the advantage of keeping costs down but also meant important places could be missed, such was the case with Sheffield when the North Midland Railway was built in the late 1830s. The line passed to the east, also missing Rotherham town centre, and a station was founded at Masborough for the opening of the first section from Derby on 11th May 1840. At this time the station was called Masborough, Rotherham, later becoming Masborough for Rotherham and Masborough & Rotherham, then finally Rotherham Masborough in 1908. From the 1960s to the 1980s the station provided Rotherham's only access to the rail network, but the location forced closure in late 1988. The building still stands and is used as an Asian restaurant.

Opposite below ROTHERHAM CENTRAL

The South Yorkshire Railway had attempted to continue the line at Mexborough through Rotherham to Tinsley, thereby opening a new route to Sheffield. However, this was opposed by the MR, which operated the Sheffield & Rotherham Railway line and the project was abandoned. After the SYR was amalgamated into the MS&LR, the company decided to press forward and build the line, but without getting permission from Parliament. After much money was spent, the line was ready for traffic in 1868 and Rotherham station opened on 1st August. This was only a temporary structure but lasted six years before being replaced. Closed in 1966, the station was reopened as Rotherham Central in 1987.

Below RYHILL

The Barnsley Coal Railway was authorised to run between Notton and Stairfoot on the Barnsley to Mexborough route. Instigated by the SYR, the scheme was subsequently taken up by the MS&LR, which succeeded in completing the line to reach Nostell on the Wakefield to Doncaster line. Ryhill was one of the few stations on the short line and opened on 1st September 1882, but was later renamed Wintersett & Ryhill in 1927. The station closed a short time later in 1930.

Above **SADDLEWORTH**

Saddleworth station, on the Leeds to Manchester line, as a LNWR 4-4-0 locomotive approaches from the west. After being taken out of service in 1968, the station became a private dwelling.

Above **RYLSTONE**
The intermediate station between Skipton and Grassington on the Yorkshire Dales Railway branch was Rylstone.

Below **SALTAIRE**
Despite being a casualty of the 'Reshaping of British Railways' report, Saltaire station has since been reopened.

Above **SANDAL & WALTON**

A late addition to the Derby to Leeds line in 1870, Sandal & Walton station was renamed Walton some 10 years before closure in 1961.

Below **SANDSEND**

View north from the south bank of Sandsend Beck to the station on the Middlesbrough to Whitby route.

Above SCARBOROUGH

The NER only made a tentative foray into the construction of railcars. At the turn of the century only two were constructed with 85 horsepower engines driving two electric motors; seating was for 48. Little success was achieved and the two were rebuilt shortly after entering service. One has been captured at Scarborough station, perhaps shortly after construction.

Opposite above SCALBY

Scalby station was the first stop on the line from Scarborough to Whitby and opened with the line. The picturesque station has since been lost underneath a housing estate.

Opposite below SCARBOROUGH SHED

LNER Gresley J39 Class 0-6-0 no. 1495 is prepared for the next duty at Scarborough shed. The locomotive was constructed at Darlington in December 1926 as part of the first batch which was ordered in 1925. Eventually the class numbered 289 and were the LNER's standard goods engine, but could also be pressed into passenger service if the need arose. Located to the south of Scarborough station, the engine shed, seen in the background, was erected by the NER in 1890 and replaced a roundhouse built only a few years earlier to the north. The former had eight tracks and these were employed up to 1963; no. 1495, as BR no. 64716, had been scrapped two years earlier.

Above SCARBOROUGH

A GCR 4-4-0 enters Scarborough station with an express, passing Falsgrave signal box. This was opened in 1907 and had 120 levers, although a proportion were taken out of use as time progressed, especially from the 1960s. The building and the signal gantry were listed during the 1980s and the box was fully restored in 2007. Only three years later a modernisation of the Scarborough station system saw the gantry and box taken out of use, with the former being removed to Grosmont on the North Yorkshire Moors Railway, whilst the latter is yet to find a new home.

Below SCHOLES

Located on the Cross Gates to Wetherby line, Scholes station was built a short distance away from the village to the north west and was due west of the larger village of Barwick in Elmet. Therefore, Scholes station was surprisingly large for the catchment area and five of the station's staff pose here for the camera with a number of passengers; there are advertising posters for Whitby and Saltburn and, interestingly, a notice board for the GNR. The station was open until 1964 and has since become a restaurant.

SCHOLES STATION

Above **SEDBERGH**
Opened by the LNWR, Sedbergh station was located on the Ingleton branch.

Below **SELBY**
A terminus station was originally opened at Selby by the Leeds & Selby Railway in 1834, but six years later when the Hull & Selby was built a through station was completed on the west side of the first one. This has subsequently been rebuilt several times.

Above **SETTLE**

In the late 1920s the LMSR was in need of a medium power express engine and the result was the Patriot Class 4-6-0s. No. 5538 *Giggleswick* was erected at Crewe in July 1933, but was not named until November 1938 - the ceremony being pictured here at Settle station.

Below **SETTRINGTON**

South east of Malton, Settrington station was the first stop on the line to Driffield.

SETTRINGTON STATION

L&Y RLY STATION SHARLSTON. S.9.

Above **SHEFFIELD MIDLAND**

MR Johnson 1400 Class 2-4-0 no. 268 at the platform of Sheffield Midland station with a passenger service. In the early 20th century improvements were made at Sheffield, one being the addition of a new island platform. Two overhead walkways were provided, one being for passengers and the other for railway employees. Recently, there has been a dispute over non-railway users accessing the overbridge which provides a shortcut to the city for tram users and residents of housing to the east.

Opposite above **SHARLSTON**

Sharlston station was opened by the L&YR c. 1870 on the line between Wakefield and Pontefract. The main building is seen (looking east) beyond the Gin Lane level crossing and the platforms are staggered. Sharlston station was close to New Sharlston colliery which connected to the line with a branch a short distance to the west, whilst Victoria colliery to the east had extensive sidings running along the route. Sharlston station closed on 3rd March 1958 but Streethouse station was opened a short distance to the east in the early 1990s.

Opposite below **SHEFFIELD MIDLAND**

The MR could not resist the allure of Sheffield for long, lest another company step in front and take the traffic from under the MR's noses. In the early 1860s the company promoted a connection from just north of Chesterfield to the former Sheffield & Rotherham Railway line at the Wicker. In true Yorkshire fashion the people of Sheffield had not forgotten the initial snub and there was not as much support for the line as the MR expected, with a rival bid being favoured, but the former was given authorisation by parliament. Further problems were encountered by the MR in buying the necessary land, though these were overcome and the line opened for traffic in 1870. Sheffield Midland station was erected on the east side of the city and over part of the River Sheaf, which was diverted into a culvert. LMS Fowler 4-4-0 compound no. 1048 is pictured at the station with an express.

Above SHERBURN-IN-ELMET

Sherburn-in-Elmet station was the final stop on the first stage of the York & North Midland Railway before reaching the Leeds & Selby Railway. The line was then extended to the NMR and the station became just one of several on the route. Located to the east of the village this view had been taken looking south to Bishopdyke Road level crossing. After closure in the 1960s the station was demolished, although a 'modern' station has since been opened and the crossing has been taken out of use.

Opposite above SHEFFIELD VICTORIA

GCR Robinson 8B Class Atlantic no. 263 (with LNER '5' prefix and classified C4 by the company) departs Sheffield Victoria station with an unidentified GCR 4-6-0 at the head of an express service. A total of 27 class members were constructed between 1903 and 1906, with no. 263 being the first of five erected by Beyer, Peacock & Co. in 1904. The 8Bs were used for many years on the important GC expresses and were only displaced towards the mid-1930s. No. 5263 was condemned in April 1949.

Opposite below SHEFFIELD VICTORIA

Sheffield Victoria station was opened in 1851 after the Manchester to Sheffield line had been extended. The facilities consisted of two island platforms with a roof over the section between the two. Up to the 20th century there were several changes and additions made, including the Victoria Hotel. LNER Thompson B1 Class 4-6-0 no. 1156 departs with the up 'South Yorkshireman' during 1948. The express ran from Bradford to London Marylebone station.

Opposite **SKELLOW SIGNAL BOX**

A GNR and GCR sign dated 1898 warns potential trespassers on the railway of a fine of 40 shillings. This is located outside Skellow signal box where the staff pose for the camera. Initially the box controlled the short spur from the fork of the West Riding & Grimsby Railway to Stainforth and the line to Doncaster which was laid in 1909. With the sinking of Bullcroft colliery, Carcroft on the north side of the line to Stainforth, the box's duties increased and the cabin was likely rebuilt; the crossing was also subsequently replaced by an overbridge.

Below **SINNINGTON**

Following the protracted construction of the line between Thirsk and Malton, thoughts turned to the area north of the line. A branch to Helmsley had been authorised but these plans were discarded and not until well into the NER's reign over the area did the route get resurrected. At first just the branch was built but then the decision was taken to extend to Kirkbymoorside, then to Pickering. Sinnington station was the only station on this latter section and was ready for traffic from 1st April 1875. NER Fletcher BTP Class 0-4-4T locomotive no. 87 is pictured at the station c. 1925 (a poster with 'LNER' and the Forth Bridge is visible). The locomotive was erected at Gateshead in October 1879 and was withdrawn in May 1927. Sinnington station was the first closure after the Second World War, being taken out of use from 2nd February 1953 and the line between Pickering and Kirkbymoorside was scrapped. The house and platform are still extant.

SKELLOW

PRIVATE

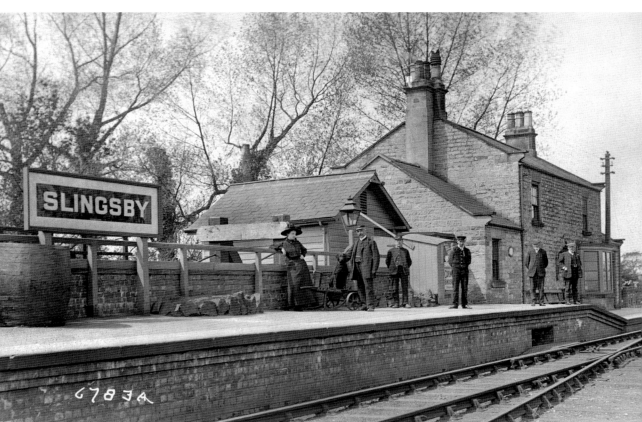

SKIPTON STATION.

SMITH

Above **SKIPTON**

Skipton station began life as the terminus of an extension of the Leeds & Bradford Railway, yet soon afterwards became a through station with the opening of the Colne route. This was the start of Skipton being an important junction in the area as other lines followed closely behind, such as the railway to Lancaster. The biggest change occurred in 1876 when the station was rebuilt a short distance away from the original site for the opening of the MR trunk route from London to Glasgow after the Settle to Carlisle line had been finished; the new station was designed by Charles Trubshaw and has since been given Grade II listed status.

Opposite above **SKELMANTHORPE**

Just over midway along the branch from Shepley, on the Huddersfield to Penistone route, and Clayton West was Skelmanthorpe station. Built on the north side of the line, this image has been captured looking in that direction from Station Road bridge, also showing the goods shed and yard. Additionally, there was a connection here, first to Nineclogs colliery, then Emley Moor Colliery when that was sunk. Whilst Skelmanthorpe station was spared closure in the 1960s, this eventually occurred in 1983 along with the branch. In the early 1990s the trackbed was reused for the Kirklees Light Railway, which opened in stages between 1991 and 1997, reaching Skelmanthorpe in 1992.

Opposite below **SLINGSBY**

Slingsby station was opened during June 1853 on the Thirsk to Malton line. Initially only a small building, several extensions were added over time, as well as a goods yard. Closure to passengers occurred in 1931 and for freight in 1964.

Left **SOOTHILL SIGNAL BOX**

Soothill signal box and several stern gentlemen pose for the camera. There were several GNR lines in the area around Soothill, north of Dewsbury, and this box perhaps belongs to the company, bearing more than a passing resemblance to Skellow signal box seen earlier.

Below **SOUTH CAVE**

Scene captured from the northern platform at South Cave station on the Hull & Barnsley Railway. The station was located a distance to the north of the village and was open from 1885 to 1955. In a state of disrepair for a number of years the station was subsequently renovated and is in private use.

Above and below SOUTH ELMSALL

Two views from opposite ends of South Elmsall station, which was opened by the West Riding & Grimsby Railway on 1st February 1866 and cost nearly £3,000. The main building was on the south side of the line, whilst a waiting shelter was on the north. Although still serving the area, the station has lost the impressive building pictured here.

Above **SPROTBROUGH**

As the Hull & Barnsley Railway's line from Wrangbrook Junction to Denaby was built for the coal traffic from the area, the fact that the passenger station at Sprotbrough only offered this service for nine years is not surprising. However, goods traffic continued to be collected at the station until the mid-1960s.

Opposite above **SOUTHCOATES**

Staff of household cleaning product manufacturers Reckitt & Sons, Hull, assemble on the platform of Southcoates station for an outing to Scarborough, c. 1905. The station was open for 100 years from 1864 and has since been demolished.

Opposite below **SPOFFORTH**

Spofforth station was briefly the terminus for the line from Church Fenton to Harrogate when construction of the final section to the latter place was delayed in 1847. Designed for the Y&NMR by G.T. Andrews, Spofforth was later closed in 1964 and demolished.

STAINTON DALE STATION

Above STAINTON DALE
Stainton Dale station on the Scarborough to Whitby line between Hayburn Wyke and Ravenscar.

Opposite above SPROTBROUGH
H&BR Stirling F2 (LNER N12) Class 0-6-2T no. 104 at Sprotbrough station, with enginemen and signalman posing for a picture. The class of nine were completed by Kitson & Co., Leeds, at the end of 1901 and were built and designed to work the colliery sidings on this section of line. In the main, the locomotives were based at Cudworth shed, but spells at Springhead, Hull, occurred and after Grouping moves deep into 'foreign' territory occurred. The majority of the N12s were withdrawn by the second half of the 1930s and no. 104 was a casualty in March 1937.

Opposite below STAINLAND
The L&YR built a branch from Greetland, near Halifax, to Stainland for industrial traffic in the mid-1870s. Even though the terminus was at Holywell Green, to the east of Stainland, the latter had the honour of the station carrying that name. This was until 1892 when Holywell Green was added for preciseness. The picture has been taken looking north to Station Road bridge, which is all that now remains of the branch, closure occurring in the late 1950s; passenger services were stopped by the LMSR in the early 1930s.

G.C. RAILWAY SMASH STAIRFOOT NOV. 21 1911

IRVING

STAIRFOOT CRASH

During the early morning of 21st November 1911 a GCR mineral train running from Stairfoot to Barnsley was derailed by the catch points in the area of Old Oaks Bridge after a broken coupling caused the train to become out of control. The line was blocked for the whole morning and passengers were obliged to alight from one train, walk past the wreckage to be taken forward by another.

STANLEY SIGNAL BOX

Signalman Wilkinson poses with the levers
inside Stanley signal box, near Wakefield,
whilst the other shot shows the exterior of the
box perhaps at an earlier date. The signal box
was located on the east side of the crossing of
Aberford Road over the Methley Joint line
between Lofthouse and Methley, with the
station located on the west side. Line, station
and signal box have since disappeared.

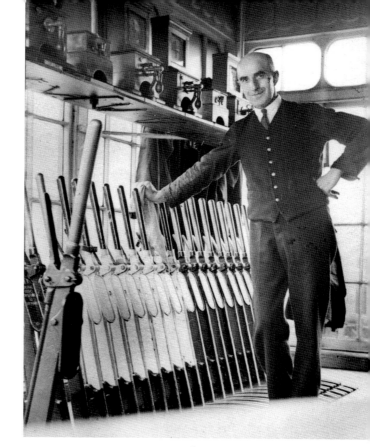

STANLEY FERRY

Coal, likely to be from St John's Colliery (also known as Newland Colliery), has been loaded into a 'Tom Pudding' at Stanley Ferry ready for transport along the Aire & Calder Navigation to Goole. Newland Colliery No. 2 - an 0-4-0ST locomotive - is providing assistance.

Above **STANLEY**
View from the west end of Stanley station to the signal box.

Below **STANNINGLEY**
A train approaches Stanningley station on the GNR's Leeds to Bradford line.

Above SWINE

View north to the Coniston Lane level crossing at Swine station on the Hull & Hornsea Railway line. Located to the east of the village (and north of Sutton-on-Hull station) Swine was unusual in having one platform located on the north side of the barriers and the other on the opposite side. The station house has remained standing after closure.

Opposite above STEETON

Looking east to Station Road crossing at Steeton & Silsden station from the platform on the south side of the line. Opened by the Leeds & Bradford Railway at the end of 1847, the station was first called Steeton, being nearer to the village than the town of Silsden, which was added to the title some 20 years later, and a distance to the north. The station continues to serve the area, but the buildings have been demolished and a bridge now carries the road over the line.

Opposite below SUTTON-ON-HULL

In the early 1860s the Hull & Hornsea Railway was promoted to bring business and tourism to the latter and this was completed by the middle of the decade. One of several wayside stations was Sutton, renamed Sutton-on-Hull in 1874, some 10 years after opening. The village was a short distance away from the edge of the city at the time of opening, but the boundary moved ever closer by the 1950s and at the present time the settlement has been enveloped. This did not improve patronage of the station and closure occurred on 19th October 1964 and the line has since been lifted.

Above **TADCASTER**
Scene captured from inside the trainshed of G.T. Andrews' station at Tadcaster.

Below **THONGS BRIDGE**
The Holmfirth branch only featured one other station - Thongs Bridge, open between 1851 and 1959.

E.R STATION. THORNE.

Above **THORNE NORTH**

The last station before the NER branch from the Hull and Selby line reached the SYR route to Doncaster was Thorne North, opened 2nd August 1869 and still serving the area.

Below **THORNER**

Scarcroft was the original name of Thorner station on the Cross Gates to Wetherby line, despite the latter being much closer; the change occurred in 1901 and lasted until closure in 1964.

Left THORNTON SIGNAL BOX

Thornton station signal box on the GNR line to Keighley with signalmen posing with a young lady, who appears to have been engaged in some decorating work, having a paint pot and brush in hand. Opened in October 1878, the station consisted of an island platform, with the signal box located on the south side.

Below TICKHILL

GCR Parker Class 2A 4-4-0 no. 688 has the honour of transporting the first passenger train, which is an excursion to Cleethorpes, on the South Yorkshire Joint Railway, departing from Tickhill station.

FIRST TRIP FROM TICKHILL STATION
JULY 6 1910.

Above TICKHILL

The official opening date of Tickhill station was not until 1st December 1910. Being a distance away from the village, usage was light and the station was permanently closed in 1929.

Below ULLESKELF

Built by the Y&NMR around 1840, Ulleskelf station continues to serve the area with trains to several cities in Yorkshire. The building has been demolished and no staff are employed.

Above **TODMORDEN**
View west from track level at Todmorden station on the Manchester & Leeds Railway line, opened 1840.

Below **WAKEFIELD WESTGATE**
Replacing an earlier station, Wakefield Westgate was opened in 1867 by the West Riding & Grimsby Railway. Unfortunately, the character of the station has been lost by the removal of the canopies and the Italianate clock tower, which stood 97 ft above the station.

Above **WAKEFIELD SHED**

L&YR Hughes steam railmotor no. 17 (as LMSR no. 10616) was the penultimate example of the type to be constructed by the company in December 1911 and was in service until November 1933. Wakefield shed was located a distance south of Kirkgate station and was open from 1893 until 1967.

Below **WAKEFIELD KIRKGATE**

Frontage of the L&YR and GNR joint station at Kirkgate, Wakefield, which was opened in 1857. The station has recently undergone a major refurbishment.

Waleswood Station   No 389

Above **WALESWOOD**

A late addition to the GCR line between Sheffield and Worksop, Waleswood was opened on 1st July 1907 to the north east of the village, but opposite the colliery of the same name. Closure occurred on 7th March 1955.

Opposite page, both pictures **WHARRAM**

Passengers and staff gather for two pictures taken c. 1930 and c. 1910.

Below **WATH CONCENTRATION YARD**

Located to the north of Wath upon Dearne, Wath concentration yard was a sprawling area for the assembly and sorting of coal wagons from the many collieries in the area. Built by the GCR, the yard cost nearly £200,000 and was opened in November 1907.

Above **WITHERNSEA**

Photograph taken from Queen Street, looking south west to Withernsea station. An NER 4-4-0 is being turned ready to be coupled to the far end of the train.

Below **WHITBY SHED**

Located to the south east of Whitby station, the locomotive shed dated from 1868.

Above **WOMBWELL**

The MR station at Wombwell was sited to the south west of the village on the Chapeltown branch; the SYR, later GCR, station was on the north east side. The former has been open for 120 years.

Below **WOMERSLEY**

Bearing a resemblance to Norton and Featherstone stations, Womersley was opened on the L&YR's Askern Branch around 1848 and was later closed by the LNER in 1947.

Above **WOODLESFORD**
An ambulance brigade formed by staff at Woodlesford station on the NMR line south of Leeds.

Below **WORTLEY**
The station at Wortley, south of Penistone, in GCR days. Closure occurred under BR in 1955.

Above **WRANGBROOK JUNCTION**

H&BR Stirling Class A (LNER Q10) no. 129 loiters at Wrangbrook Junction between Kirk Smeaton and Upton on the H&BR main line. At this point the two lines to Wath and Denaby made their way south.

Below **YORK**

NER W. Worsdell Class R (LNER D20) 4-4-0 no. 2018 heads south out of York station past the locomotive sheds on the left and the old engine repair shops on the right. The original Y&NMR station was located a short distance behind the latter and was replaced by the new through station in 1877.

Below **YORK**

A favourite spot for many a photographer was York Holgate/Racecourse platform just south of the station, with a large proportion taken looking back to York, Holgate Road Bridge and St Paul's Church. The platform was only used intermittently from 1860 to the start of the Second World War for traffic arriving in the city for special occasions and race meetings. NER W. Worsdell P1 Class (LNER J25) no. 525 is seen travelling south with a coal train.

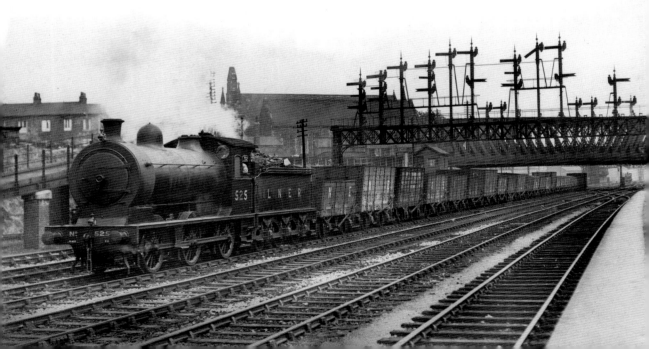

Above **YORK**

Worsdell's R Class 4-4-0s were developed at the end of the 19th century to cope with the increasing demands on the motive power from heavier trains. High boiler pressure with large cylinders were used, in addition to piston valves, which had been perfected by the company for several years previously. The first ten were constructed in 1899 and a further ten followed in 1900, the first being no. 2021, pictured, which was turned out from Gateshead in August. The class were found more than capable on the expresses operating from the main cities in Yorkshire and the north east and were only displaced from these duties after Grouping with the introduction of Gresley's designs. No. 2021 was one of the early withdrawals as the class became surplus to requirements and was condemned in December 1947.

BIBLIOGRAPHY

Dow, George. *Great Central – Volumes 1 – 3.*
Fawcett, Bill. *A History of North Eastern Railway Architecture – Volumes 1 – 3.*
Fawcett, Bill. *George Townsend Andrews of York: The Railway Architect.*
Goode, C.T. *Railways in South Yorkshire.*
Griffiths, Roger and Paul Smith. *The Directory of British Engine Sheds and Principal Locomotive Servicing Points: 2 North Midlands, Northern England and Scotland.*
Hawkins, Chris and George Reeve. *LMS Engine Sheds Volume 2: The Midland Railway.*
Hoole, K. *Railways in the Yorkshire Dales.*
Hoole, K. *A Regional History of the Railways of Great Britain Volume 4: The North East.*
Joy, David. *A Regional History of the Railways of Great Britain Volume 8: South and West Yorkshire.*
Lane, Barry C. *Lancashire and Yorkshire Railway Locomotives.*
Quick, Michael. *Railway Passenger Stations in Great Britain: A Chronology.*
RCTS. *Locomotives of the LNER Part 2B.*
RCTS. *Locomotives of the LNER Part 3A.*
RCTS. *Locomotives of the LNER Part 3B.*
RCTS. *Locomotives of the LNER Part 3C.*
RCTS. *Locomotives of the LNER Part 5.*
RCTS. *Locomotives of the LNER Part 6A.*
RCTS. *Locomotives of the LNER Part 6C.*
RCTS. *Locomotives of the LNER Part 7.*
RCTS. *Locomotives of the LNER Part 9A.*
RCTS. *Locomotives of the LNER Part 9B.*
Wrottesley, John. *The Great Northern Railway – Volumes 1 – 3.*

Also available from Great Northern by Peter Tuffrey

The Last Days of Scottish Steam

The Last Years of Yorkshire Steam

Gresley's A3s

visit *www.greatnorthernbooks.co.uk* for details.